THE LEADERSHIP GPS

*Your Turn by Turn Guide To
Becoming A Successful Leader And
Changing Lives Along The Way*

Denis G. McLaughlin

CONTENTS

INTRODUCTION

BRIAN AND HIS GRANDFATHER

Friday at 7:00 p.m., Brian Alden was sitting in his car in the parking lot at work after another long week. He was thinking about his grandfather, Michael Tennyson. He missed their long talks; they saw life the same way. His mom still tells him that he and her dad were two of a kind. Brian's grandfather was very successful, although not successful in the way most people define success. He wasn't what you would call wealthy, but he always seemed comfortable in a financial way and never talked about needing anything. He was an entrepreneur who started many businesses. He said, "Being part of person's life while they achieve their purpose by helping them identify, develop, and make full use of their strengths was my success."

Before he died, they used to solve all of the toughest problems together, often sharing a story that illustrated the problem, and the solution, just right. He would say, "You can learn a lot from other people's successes and failures. The wise person will follow another's success and avoid the failure." Brian was in dire need of one of those stories now.

The problem Brian was facing was too big and too difficult to be solved alone. It wasn't that he hadn't paid attention and remembered the stories; he remembered them all. But that was part of the problem. Which story out of the hundreds should he use now? Or were there several stories that could be used? If there were several, in what order should they be used? Grandfather would pick just the right story, and Brian needed the right answer, not just an answer. He remembered two of those difficult times from the past.

The first time was when he was seven. He joined little league baseball. The league was hoping that one of the fathers would volunteer to coach the team that Brian was on, but no one did. Without a coach his team would be disbanded; he and his friends would not be able to play that year.

Brian and his grandfather talked about Joshua Chamberlain, the leader of the Twentieth Maine regiment in the Battle of Gettysburg. Chamberlain and his soldiers were the sole protectors for the left flank of the Union army. The number of his troops was low, the regiment sustained many casualties, and they were almost completely out of ammunition. With no one to offer help, he could accept defeat or take matters into his own hands. He chose to not accept defeat. He ordered his troops to charge the Confederate army with their bayonets in the air. Against all odds, one hundred Confederate soldiers surrendered and the left flank of the Union army was saved. Chamberlain said, "The cause for which we fought was higher, our thought wider...that thought was our power."

Brian knew just what to do. He would not accept defeat. If no one else would coach, he would take matters into his own hands. He would be the coach. The team came together for practice. Some arrived on their bikes; others were dropped off by their moms. They held their first practice. At the next practice, two dads showed up and volunteered to coach.

The second time was when he was in fifth grade. His school decided to experiment with different styles of teaching. His class was selected to receive cardboard boxes to store their books in instead of desks. Since they didn't have desks, they could sit anywhere in the room they wanted. This was all pretty fun until about halfway through the year, when everyone's boxes began to wear out. The tops fell off and there were tears in the sides. This experiment was not going well at all.

One day the teacher announced that the students would have to pay to replace their boxes. This wasn't a rich school. Many of the families didn't have extra money to cover this type of cost, and the class didn't have a say in this new teaching style. He went to his grandfather and shared his dilemma.

They talked about Edmund Burke. He was a member of the British Parliament before and during the American Revolution. Known for his staunch support for the British Parliament, he nonetheless sided with the American colonies on the right to fair representation on taxation. When the Stamp Act and then the Tea Act were passed, causing the Boston Tea Party in December 1773, Burke saw that someone needed to take action to avert what were soon to be larger issues. In April 1774, he gave a speech in Parliament in which he argued that Britain should maintain peace and end these unfair taxes. Grandfather finished by quoting Burke and said, "The only thing necessary for evil to triumph is for good men to do nothing."

Brian knew just what he should do. He took this situation to the principal and explained that the experiment had not worked, and the additional cost to the students in his class was not fair. The principal ended the experiment and brought the desks back into the room.

BRIAN'S JOB

Brian graduated from college a few years ago with a degree in computer science. He has a gift for understanding computer technology; it seems to come naturally. He can't remember a time when he didn't have a computer and the latest technology as soon as it was on the market. He was one of those kids who camped outside the electronics store to buy the first iPhone and iPad. He understands the possibilities of computer technology and the limitations if it isn't built correctly. So of course his first job out of college, the one he still has today, was in computer programming at SBC Technology, a medium-size computer software company. Until thirty days before, he was the lead programmer for one of the accounting packages for small businesses. Then he was promoted to be the manager of all accounting software for the company's small-business division.

He received this promotion, in part, because he was a very good lead programmer. His job as the lead programmer was to direct the design and coding of any new enhancements that were given to the team by his manager. He was good at this not just because he excels at software design and programming himself, but because he genuinely enjoys helping other people succeed. He liked the brainstorming sessions he led with the other programmers in his area, especially the times when he saw the eyes of one of the programmers light up when they had an idea so great they started fidgeting, almost bouncing, in their seat wanting to share it. Grandfather would call this "the bouncing before the announcing."

The other reason he received this promotion, actually probably the main reason, was that Lloyd Henry, the head of the small-business division, announced his retirement and Brian's boss, Arthur Richmond, was promoted to be the new head of the small-business division.

The small-business division was well known to generate the most sales at SBC Technology and Lloyd was well compensated for this success—nice suits, nice cars, nice home. No one thought he shouldn't have been well paid; he started this division and made it what it is today.

He was a very likable person, always had a smile when you saw him in meetings. He ran the division in an interesting way. He said, "I am the idea man" at his regularly scheduled monthly rallies, where he would bring the entire division together for a thirty-minute pep talk. He would talk about his next big idea for software and then say, "You are all the experts and I trust you to deliver on my ideas," for the closing remark of the rally each month. Then he would disappear until the next rally.

At first, Brian thought, "Is that all? What am I supposed to do with that? Does he really think we can deliver a new software program every month? Doesn't he realize that there are methods, protocols, rules for developing and releasing new software?" But somehow the division kept making sales, so the team settled into a rhythm of just getting the new software out as quickly as they could.

Arthur had a different management style. While Lloyd liked to drop an idea and leave, Arthur was not an "idea man." He was good at execution; he got things done. He focused on his team's success. Brian could recite the words he heard so often, "We have been given a job to do, and we will do it just as it was written." There was actually a poster with that motto on the wall behind Arthur's desk.

Whenever anyone suggested a change to a project, he would lean over his desk and say, "Do you see those words behind me? Those words are what made me successful, and I am not going to change what makes me successful."

BRIAN'S DILEMMA

Brian stared out of the driver's side window of his car, looking at the entrance to SBC Technology. Monday morning he would be walking through those doors again to start his second month as the manager of small-business accounting software.

That title made it sound as if he knew how to manage the team developing small-business accounting software. He didn't. It had been thirty days and he was no further ahead than the day his promotion was announced. He could picture the look on the faces of his new team the day his promotion was announced. They expected him to say something wise, something uplifting. They were like a football team in the locker room at halftime, and they wanted to know the game plan. What was their coach going to tell them to do? Brian wished he knew.

As he turned his gaze back into his car, the GPS caught his attention. He had never driven his car without it in the front window; he was so used to it being there that he almost didn't even notice it anymore. But today it seemed to stand out more than he remembered. It was a gift from his grandfather, who had taught him to drive. He reached into his glove compartment and pulled out the card that came with this gift to read the message again: "Now you understand how to drive. Each time you enter your car, you will have a destination in mind. Some of those destinations will be harder to reach than others. For those destinations that are the hardest, for the routes you have not traveled before, use this GPS as your guide, following the path that others have taken successfully before you."

He read the final sentence again out loud. "'For those destinations that are the hardest, for the routes you have not traveled before, use this GPS as your guide.' Well, this leadership destination certainly is one of the harder ones; I haven't traveled this path before."

As Brian reached to type in the destination SUCCESSFUL LEADERSHIP, where he hoped to arrive someday, he caught himself thinking, "This can't work." But what did he have to lose? The worst thing that could happen is the familiar voice that had guided his driving along new paths for the last few years would say, "Destination not found."

BRIAN'S SOLUTION

He typed in SUCCESSFUL LEADERSHIP and pressed GO. What came back was a voice he knew very well, but it wasn't the voice of the GPS.

"Congratulations, Brian," said the voice of his grandfather. "You have just taken the first step on what promises to be an exciting journey to successful leadership development." After a long pause, Grandfather continued, "You are probably wondering why you are hearing my voice through these speakers."

"Not really," Brian thought.

He had learned early on not to question his grandfather's wisdom or his methods of imparting knowledge. Anyone who was fortunate enough to be mentored by his grandfather would just trust that he would lead them to the right answer for whatever situation they were in; and he always did.

"I am speaking to you through the GPS for two reasons. The lessons that you will learn about leadership are the same lessons you learned when I taught you to drive. We will travel through the same ten lessons we enjoyed together when it was time for you to master driving.

"The other reason is that I know you understand the inner workings of this technology. You know that there are twenty-four satellites orbiting the earth twice a day that enable your position to be pinpointed through triangulation. You understand the complicated algorithms that are run to direct the user to their chosen destination. Most important, you understand that at the root of these technological wonders is the basic map. These maps were drawn and are updated by individuals who have traveled these routes and recorded their paths. This is how this GPS has been able to anticipate and direct each turn you needed to make; it has the knowledge of successful drivers programmed into it. I have studied the routes of successful leaders and recorded their paths. This knowledge has been programmed into your

GPS. Now it can also anticipate and direct each turn you need to make to reach your destination of successful leadership."

He started the car and headed home. It was getting late. He was hungry, and he needed to prepare for the weekend. Monday was coming fast and he knew he was going to learn leadership from the best. This weekend would be like studying for finals in school: little sleep, lots of coffee, load up on knowledge. The morning meetings at SBC were Brian's tests and he planned on getting straight *A*s.

CHAPTER ONE

WHENEVER POSSIBLE, FOLLOW THE ROAD MORE TRAVELED.

Brian woke up early Saturday morning excited to learn all he could about successful leadership. He showered, shaved, dressed, and had a slice of toast. He started the coffee brewing, walked over to his desk, and looked at the picture of him and his grandfather taken the day he passed his driver's license test. Next to the picture on his desk were the GPS and his laptop where he would take notes on everything he learned.

He turned on the GPS, typed SUCCESSFUL LEADERSHIP and pressed GO. "Good morning, Brian," came Grandfather's voice once again.

He breathed a sigh of relief that this was really happening and wasn't just the result of the last thirty days of stress and sleep deprivation.

"This journey to successful leadership began when I said that we will travel through the same ten lessons we enjoyed together when it was time for you to master driving. How could driving lessons help anyone learn leadership? In my many years in business, I discovered that most people are genuinely convinced that their situations are so unique and so difficult that no one has faced quite the same circumstances before, let alone found a way to solve them. In some ways, I think it is a bit of pride in the human condition that makes people want a difficult solution for their difficult problems. But it doesn't need to be difficult. Eighty percent of most problems have been solved before; the other

20 percent is taking the initiative to accept the solution given to you and implementing it.

"Take, for instance, Marcus Aurelius, the Roman emperor from 161 AD to 180 AD, who is best known for protecting the Roman Empire from invasions by the Parthians and the Germans. He once said, 'Because a thing seems difficult for you, do not think it impossible for anyone to accomplish.'

"Then there is Thomas Edison, the holder of 1,093 Unites States patents and the inventor of the phonograph and the incandescent light bulb. He said, 'Keep on the outlook for novel and interesting ideas that others have used successfully. Your idea has to be original only in its adaptation to the problem you are currently working on.'"

Brian stopped the GPS and started typing his summary of what he'd just heard: *My job is to do it the right way, not to invent the right way.*

THE THREE PHASES OF LEADERSHIP

Brian pressed GO on the GPS, and Grandfather continued. "The first lesson you will learn on leadership is called the Three Phases of Leadership. Before we get into the details of the ten steps of successful leadership and driving, I want to tell you the story of what I learned about leadership through the game of golf. You may remember some of the stories your mother told you about her brother and me, and the fun we had golfing together as he grew up.

"I learned about the Three Phases of Leadership over many years. I started golfing with my older brother when I was about ten years old. Since my brother and I were a twosome, the starters on the course always found two other players to join us to make a foursome. Most of the time, the two other players were older gentlemen. The starters always used to say that foursomes speed up play.

"I can tell you from experience that two young boys can race around the course much faster than two young boys paired with two older men. I was pretty sure that the real reason was to slow down our playing so the older gentlemen could enjoy their game.

"These older gentlemen would instruct us after every shot. They always started by saying that 'golf is not a race' and that we should 'slow down and enjoy the scenery and the walk.' I found it puzzling that these gentlemen, who couldn't hit the ball any farther or straighter than either my brother or I, and had just spent the afternoon giving us advice on each shot, would always leave the course with a smile and a handshake, saying they enjoyed golfing with us and reminding us of that one hole, or sometimes a single shot, that one of us had played well. I remember those many gentlemen today. They taught me that when you are teaching someone something new, slow down, enjoy the process, and celebrate the small successes.

"The first phase of leadership is RELATIONSHIP. The relationship built through leadership is remembered long after understanding and knowledge are imparted.

"As I became an adult, I decided that it was time to raise my golf game to a new level. No longer was breaking one hundred going to be good enough. I remembered reading that if you want to hit great shots, you have to picture great shots in your mind before you swing. I didn't know what great shots really looked like at that point, so I reached out to the experts who had done this before to be my guides.

"I bought books and videos by champion professional golfers. I attended local pro golf tournaments to see what great golfers looked like and even to hear how they sounded. Professional golf had just started airing on television, so I began watching the professional golfers with intentional focus on their swings. I was persistent and spent many evenings at the driving range practicing. In time, I became an accomplished amateur golfer who could play well on any course.

"The second phase of leadership is UNDERSTANDING. The understanding of what success looks like comes from modeling yourself after those who have successfully achieved the outcome you desire.

"Several years later I was married, and your uncle was born. As he grew and became ready for his first set of real golf clubs at around age seven, I decided it was time that he and I venture out to golf together. I was determined to teach him all I had learned about golf. I would enjoy the relationship that would develop as I taught him, as I had learned from the older gentlemen in my early days. I would share an understanding of what success looked like when I taught him the grip, stance, and swing that I had learned from observing the professionals.

"Your uncle caught on well; in no time he could hit with every one of the four clubs in his bag (driver, seven iron, nine iron and putter). He was ready to venture from the driving range and head for the par-three golf courses. I couldn't wait. The first hole was 140 yards long. I hit my shot and told him it was his turn to show me all he had learned. He stared with a puzzled look, not really wanting to ask the question that he had on the tip of his tongue. 'What club should I use?' he asked. I answered, 'The driver, of course.' He had a beautiful swing and the ball traveled about 120 yards. When we approached his ball for his second shot, he again asked 'What club should I use now?' 'Your nine iron,' I said, 'using the windmill pitch.' Again his shot was just as he had learned at the driving range, and it rolled near the cup. He approached the ball on the green and asked what club he should use.

"This pattern of asking which club to use at almost every turn continued for all nine holes and for several more outings. At this point I realized that while I had taught him *how* to hit each golf club, I had not given him the knowledge of *when* to use each club. I also realized that the only way I could teach him when to hit each club was for me to walk alongside him and use every opportunity to teach him.

"The third phase of leadership is KNOWLEDGE. The knowledge of when to apply what is understood comes through the side-by-side journey of mentorship. You may think that I invented these three phases of leadership, but it is more accurate to say I discovered them. I make a point of saying 'discovered,' because they were there all along.

"When I was in high school, my science teacher taught a lesson on the human brain and memory. There were three phases to learning, which she called the think principle: think about what you are being taught and see how to do it right, think and then do it right, do it right without thinking.

"I would say that my high school science teacher discovered the three phases for herself, but they existed long before I was in high school. In my study of leadership, I came across an ancient Chinese proverb that describes the three phases like this: tell me and

I will forget; show me and I may remember; involve me and I will comprehend.

"I can tell you that the three phases of leadership worked for me in my career, and I know they will work for you. I lived them out for many years, but my lifetime of experience pales in comparison to the thousands of years that they have been in existence. I can't say when they were developed, but I can say that they have been used by many a great leader who would be proud to know that I am passing them on to you."

Brian had started typing as soon as he heard Grandfather say there were three phases of leadership. He wanted to make sure he would catch the phases and the lessons that would be taught in each phase. He was trying to remember the ten lessons that Grandfather used to teach him to drive, but that was almost nine years ago, and he wasn't taking notes then, he was keeping his hands on the wheel as he would need to do if he wanted to pass the driver's test. He did get the three phases of leadership typed out just before Grandfather resumed his lesson—relationship, understanding, and knowledge.

"The examples of the three phases of leadership are three versions of the same message given to three people at three points in history to address three different needs for leadership. Each one led the recipients down the same path using a language they could understand, a parable if you will. I am using the driving lessons as our parable to share the message with you; it is a language that you understand.

"You must remember that as the phases of the moon influence the rising of the tides during spring, summer, fall and winter, the three phases of leadership will influence your success in all seasons of your career. And as the phases of the moon move in a predetermined order every month, the three phases of leadership must move in their prescribed order.

"Phase one is the foundation for all you will do and accomplish, but it is a complex phase. Without success in phase one you will not be able to move forward through the next two phases. You and your team may be frustrated because you cannot accomplish more than you can personally direct. Conversely, with success in phase one you will be tempted to stop moving forward and miss reaping the benefits of changing lives in a big way.

"There will be lives changed in phase one, but that is just the beginning; it can be so much more. Phase one will prepare you and your team for the next two phases. Phases two and three build on the success of phase one. These two phases prepare your team members for their ultimate opportunity for personal success: becoming leaders of their own teams.

"Admiral James B. Stockdale, one of the most highly decorated officers in the history of the United States Navy, summed up the results of the three phases of leadership. He said, 'What we need for leaders are men of the heart who are so helpful that they, in effect, do away with the need for their jobs. But leaders like that are never out of a job, never out of followers. Strange as it sounds, great leaders gain authority by giving it away.'

"This quote is especially impactful if you know the life of Admiral James B. Stockdale. He was the very definition of a successful leader throughout his career. He was an instructor in the US Naval Test Pilot School, a commander of a navy fighter squadron, and in his most successful leadership role in my opinion, he was the highest ranking prisoner of war during the Vietnam War for seven years. During this time he was tortured, malnourished, and held in solitary confinement for long periods of time. He continued to lead his fellow prisoners by developing a method of secret communication to share encouraging philosophies that empowered them to achieve their goal: survival."

Brian turned off the GPS. He was going to be part of the long history of leaders dating back thousands of years who had followed a well-worn path. Building a successful team and changing lives was exactly what he had hoped to accomplish. But was he ready for this responsibility?

It didn't matter if he thought he was ready or not; he already had the responsibility. If Grandfather recorded these maps on the GPS for him, then he must have believed that Brian could be successful if he followed the right path.

THE THREE PHASES OF LEADERSHIP

Phase One	Phase Two	Phase Three
Relationship	Understanding	Knowledge
Think and See	Think and Do	Do without Thinking
Tell Me	Show Me	Involve Me

PHASE ONE—RELATIONSHIP

The Relationship Built Through Leadership Is Remembered Long After Understanding and Knowledge Are Imparted.

CHAPTER TWO

WHERE ARE YOU GOING?

FOLLOWERS DON'T FOLLOW UNTIL THEY TRUST LEADERS TO LEAD.

Brian grabbed a bottle of water and settled back down at his desk to learn, one phase at a time and one step at a time. He turned on the GPS, and Grandfather picked up where he left off.

"I called phase one "Relationship." Why is establishing a relationship so important as you seek to be a successful leader? That question can be answered by reviewing the content of phase one in the two other examples of the three phases of leadership.

"The ancient Chinese proverb said phase one is 'Tell me and I will forget.' My high school science teacher said phase one is 'Think about what you are being taught and see how to do it right.'

"The two main words to focus on in those examples of the three phases of leadership are: TELL and SEE. In phase one you will be establishing your influence as a leader so that your team will follow you when you TELL them the way, and they SEE the way you will be taking them. The only way you can establish the influence you need is to establish the trust your team needs. And only through a relationship can you establish trust. Trying to influence another person without first establishing trust is like trying to boil water outside of a kettle. Trust, like the kettle, is the vessel in which all things work together to generate powerful action.

"When you and I began your driving lessons we had a relationship already established. You trusted that I had your best interests at heart because of our relationship. You trusted that I knew how to drive because of our relationship and that I could teach you how to drive because of our relationship. As you begin your journey into a leadership role, you most likely don't yet have a relationship with your team. Without an established relationship, you will not yet have trust, and without trust, your team will not follow your leadership."

Brian did trust his grandfather to teach him to drive for the very reason he just said: their relationship. They had spent a lifetime together and whenever Brian had a problem, his grandfather's advice always worked. That is why he didn't hesitate for a moment to drive home last night, get a good night's sleep, and start that very morning to become a great leader under his expert mentor.

STEP ONE: WHERE ARE YOU GOING?

Grandfather continued, "There are five steps in phase one. Each step is part of the path that strengthens the relationship you're building that will lead to the trust you need in order to lead. The first step in being a successful leader is to understand your team's purpose. How is success defined for the team you are now leading? Before you begin to lead a team, you need to define success for your team so that you and your team members will understand when you are successful.

"Do you remember the first phrase I taught you when we began your driving lessons? It was the phrase we repeated together at the beginning of each journey, until you said it on your own before I could ask."

"You have to know where you're going. If you don't know where you're going, you'll never know if you've arrived," they said in unison.

Brian laughed, and then sighed a deep, warm sigh. It felt good to have that connection again, even if only for a few seconds. He wrote that phrase down and turned back to listen to the rest of step one.

"When I taught you how to drive, that phrase made perfect sense. Before you drive a car, you have to know where you're going. Without knowing where you're going you won't even know which direction to turn out of the driveway, let alone which roads to take. It makes a difference if you're going to drive to the corner store for bread or if you're going to drive across the country on a vacation.

"Leadership is no different from driving. You have to know where you're going—your purpose as a team—or you risk not getting there. In all areas of leadership, purpose matters.

"Dwight Eisenhower was a successful leader in the military as the United States Commanding General of the victorious European forces during World War Two. He was also a successful leader in education as the president of Columbia University after the war. He is best known for his success as a leader, serving two terms as the thirty-fourth president of the United States. In talking about purpose, Eisenhower said, 'We succeed only as we identify in life, or in war, or in anything else, a single overriding objective, and make all other considerations bend to that one objective.'

"Vince Lombardi, the former head coach of the Green Bay Packers, successfully led the team during the 1960s, when they dominated the league. Lombardi's Packers won five league championships in seven years, including the first two Super Bowls. In speaking about purpose, Lombardi said, 'Success demands singleness of purpose.'

"Daniel Boone, the famous pioneer, fought in the Revolutionary War, settled the Commonwealth of Kentucky before it joined the Union, and served as a state assemblyman after the war. He said, 'Having an exciting destination is like setting a needle in your compass. From then on, the compass knows only one point: its ideal. And it will faithfully guide you there through the darkest nights and fiercest storms.'

"All of these successful leaders in various fields said, in various ways, the exact same thing I said to you when we first started your driving lessons: 'You have to know where you're going. If you don't know where you're going, you'll never know if you've arrived.' Brian, just like these great leaders, you need to understand the single purpose for your team."

PHASE ONE—RELATIONSHIP
The Relationship Built Through Leadership is Remembered Long After Understanding and Knowledge are Imparted.

Step One: Where are you going?

You have to know where you're going. If you don't know where you're going, you'll never know if you've arrived.

CHAPTER THREE

WHAT ARE THE CONDITIONS?

THE MOST SUCCESSFUL LEADER IS THE ONE WITH THE BEST INFORMATION.

Brian let the GPS stay on so he could continue learning the steps to successful leadership. He didn't want to take a break. The similarity of knowing where you are going in the car to knowing where you are going in leadership made perfect sense to him. He quickly got a bowl of pretzels and a glass of lemonade from the kitchen and sat back down.

"Benjamin Disraeli was a prominent member of the British government during the 1800s. He served in leadership positions for three decades including twice as prime minister. In addition, he was an accomplished author."

As Grandfather talked, Brian remembered how they used to have snacks on the porch and discuss historical leaders. It was as if that person were right there with them, rocking in their chair, sipping lemonade, and smiling.

"Shortly after the Union victory in the American Civil War in 1865, voices for expanding voting rights and participation in government by all people became stronger in Britain. Disraeli understood this shift in feeling, and using that information, he persuaded his Conservative Party to pass the 1867 Reform Act, which expanded the right to vote to the urban, working-class males. This was the beginning of a renewed Conservative

Party, which brought such great leaders as Winston Churchill and Margaret Thatcher.

"Today, Disraeli is thought of as one of the driving forces behind the Conservative Party. How did he do all he did?

"Disraeli said, 'The secret of success in life is for a man to be ready for his opportunity when it comes.' He also said, 'The more extensive a man's knowledge of what has been done, the greater will be his power of knowing what to do.'

"The life of Benjamin Disraeli teaches us that we must be prepared to make decisions by having the best information available at all times. This leads us to step two of phase one. The successful leader knows the conditions in and around his team."

STEP TWO: WHAT ARE THE CONDITIONS?

It was approaching late afternoon. The morning had gone by fast, and Brian had missed lunch. He was not about to stop now; he wanted to hear about step two. He let Grandfather continue.

"Take yourself back to your driving lessons. Before you could take any action to get where you're going, I said, you need to understand the conditions you will be driving in and the condition of your car. No matter how short or long your journey, always consider the current weather and the future forecast. Step two is called 'What Are the Conditions?'

"Now, you can't affect the weather, but you can act according to its potential impacts. If it is summer, you don't have to worry about snow and ice on the road. If your journey is to the corner store in the spring, then your weather forecast can be obtained by just going outside and smelling the air for rain to see if you should bring along an umbrella. But if you are planning a cross-country drive in January, then you have much more research to undertake. It may be cold where you live, with no snow on the ground, but that may not hold true for the states you will travel through, or your final destination.

"The best drivers will know the forecasts all along the way so they can set their route to avoid bad weather, and they will keep track of changing forecasts to alter their route if necessary once they begin. Keep in mind that the depth of your research on external conditions will be determined by the complexity of your journey and the pace of change around you."

Brian had taken that advice to heart when he learned how to drive. It had become part of his routine to check the forecast each morning on his iPhone so he knew what the day's weather would be like.

"Now on to the condition of your car," Grandfather continued. "This is one of those pieces of information that you will always have to know, no matter the length of your journey. These are the conditions that you can affect. There are some conditions that are easy to monitor—the fuel level, the tire pressure. There are other conditions that take some work and some expense to maintain correctly and will remain hidden until you examine them or they stop working—brake linings, fuel filters, engine oil quality, or tire tread. These are conditions that should never be allowed to fail; you should plan to have them checked by professionals and replaced on schedule."

Brian remembered this conversation as well. He never let the gas tank drop below half and he quickly looked at all of his tires before driving. He kept a journal in his car to log all the maintenance items that had been completed and his dealership texted him with all upcoming scheduled maintenance. He was a well-prepared driver, but how could he relate this to leadership? There was only one way to find out: return to the GPS.

"I said that step two in successful leadership is to know the conditions in and around your team. In our driving analogy, the weather is the economy and your industry, and the car is your team.

"The economy and your industry are the conditions that happen around your team. As with the weather you will be unable to control these conditions, but you can act to reduce their impact. In order to adapt according to the economy and your industry, you have to understand them.

"Just as when you drive, no matter how short or how long your leadership journey may be, you have to take into consideration the current conditions and the future forecast. What is the state of the general economy? Is it growing? Are consumers and businesses buying? Or is the economy struggling, and consumer and business sentiment poor? Like the weather, this is a changing condition that must be monitored. There are seasons to the economy when you can feel content and warm, but there are also seasons when, if you are unprepared, you will find yourself on the side of the road, having slid into a ditch. These conditions don't tend to change rapidly unless you are in volatile times such as a recession.

"What about your industry? Are there a few tough competitors who control the market, or is there room for innovation and new ideas? If you stay tuned in to these conditions you will be able to act early and mitigate their impact on your team.

"Remember that the depth of your research on external conditions will be determined by the complexity of your journey and the pace of change around you.

"Now, on to your team—the condition you can control. As with the car you drive, the condition of your team is one of those pieces of information that you will have to always know, no matter the length of your journey. There are some conditions that should be easy to monitor. You should always know if your team is successful. In order to do that, you need to complete step one, "Where Are You Going?" Once you do that, you simply check your reports, which you may need to develop to track your progress toward your goals. Like the gas gauge or tire pressure, you need to look at this on a regular basis to ensure you don't get off track.

"There are other conditions that are harder to monitor and will take time and expense to maintain in proper working order, such as morale. Monitor the morale of your team. Do they like their work? Are they satisfied with their co-workers? Are they satisfied with their opportunities for advancement? You can—and should—talk to your team regularly and ask these questions. You may receive an individual complaint, which may be an indication of a larger issue, just as you may hear a squeaking brake, which may mean something is wrong with your car.

"The most successful companies work with professionals to administer anonymous surveys. These surveys ask specific questions to all team members and provide analysis of key opportunities for improvement along with pointing out areas that are working well. New leaders are sometimes surprised to learn that no matter how well their team is performing, and no matter how much their team likes them as a leader, the team members are hesitant to tell the new leader what could be improved in one-on-one conversation. All of this information is necessary to navigate a team through the current external conditions and prepare them for future external conditions."

Brian was still typing notes, capturing all that Grandfather said. He would need these notes to refer to as he put into practice what he was learning. Only two steps and he already had pages of notes. It was getting close to dinnertime and he was ready to take a break, eat, and think about all he had learned today. But something pulled him back to the GPS one more time. He waited for Grandfather to start talking about step three.

ASSIGNMENT

"When you start something new, the beginning is the most difficult part. Sir Isaac Newton's first law of motion states, 'A body at rest will remain at rest unless an outside force acts on it, and a body in motion will remain in motion unless acted upon by an outside force.' Now that you are in motion, this will become easier to understand with each new step and each new phase. In leadership, you will find that the more you grow, the further you are able to go. I am not going to continue teaching you the five steps in phase one just yet. It is time for you to complete some homework. Only your homework will have to be completed in the office.

"When you were learning how to drive, I gave you this same homework at the same time. Your homework assignment is to research and understand steps one and two of your leadership assignment, just as I asked you to research and understand steps one and two of driving your car.

"Step one, deciding where you're going, was easy homework when you learned how to drive; you just decided. For your leadership assignment it won't be as simple as just deciding.

"The same applies to step two, understanding the conditions in and around your team. It will take more work to understand the economy, your industry, and your team than it did the weather and your car. It will take more work, but there have been great leaders who have laid the path for how this work is done successfully.

"When you research the economy and your industry, think about the path of George Washington Carver. He attended Iowa State University in the 1890s and obtained his bachelor's and master's degree in botany.

He went on to the African American Tuskegee Institute, where he taught and performed research. The Tuskegee agriculture department became well known for its innovations in crop rotation and alternate crops such as peanuts. Carver started a mobile teaching program where he brought his knowledge to local farmers, who implemented his new methods.

"The highly educated George Washington Carver said, 'Reading about nature is fine, but if a person walks in the woods and listens carefully, he can learn more than what is in books…'

"Your homework on the economy and your industry will involve research using today's tools like the internet where there is abundant information. As Carver advised, you should also seek out and listen to leaders in your industry who can talk about their experience with these conditions.

"When you inspect your team, follow the path of Michael Abrashoff. He was the Commander of the USS Benfold in the late 1990s. Under Abrashoff's command, the USS Benfold went from being rated as the worst ship in the navy to the best ship in the navy.

"When Abrashoff joined the ship, he wanted to understand why the ship was rated so poorly. He read two surveys. One was a survey of sailors who had left the navy; one was a survey of the current sailors on the Benfold. Each survey gave insight into potential problems. But Abrashoff had a saying by which he led: 'The most important thing that a commander can do is to see the ship from the eyes of the crew.' Abrashoff took the time to personally interview each of his 310 crewmembers and ask them what should change.

"Each of these leaders understood that the most successful leader is the one with the best information. The best information comes through looking, listening, and learning. You look for information that already exists in books, surveys, or websites; you listen to people with information gained through experience; and you learn what people need by analyzing the two together.

"Before I send you on to complete your assignment, I have one more piece of advice that has guided my career in each company I started.

"There are three constituents in your company whose support you need for your leadership role to be successful: your team, your investors, and your customers. Each of these has different needs and each can provide information about the conditions in and around your team.

"First, a company is nothing more than the joining together of the multiple teams of people. I think of the teams as the body. Without the teams there is no body and no company. Teams provide the means for the work to be done. They want an environment in which they can survive and grow.

"Second, a body needs food for energy. Your investors, who could be your boss, the owner, or the shareholders, provide the energy for the teams in the form of budget dollars. All of these investors seek a profitable return on their investment.

"Third, a body needs oxygen to breathe. Your customers provide the oxygen for the company when they purchase your product. Your customers look for a product that meets their needs. When you return from your homework assignment you should have information you obtained about the experience and needs of each of these three constituents.

"This is an important assignment. The information you gather by looking, listening, and learning will be that on which you base all future steps to successful leadership."

Brian turned off the GPS and closed his laptop. He had learned a lot but there was more to learn on his own. He took a piece of paper from his notebook and wrote two questions: *What is the purpose of my team? What are the conditions in and around my team?*

These two questions were his first assignment. He thought back to the night before, when he'd first heard Grandfather's voice through the GPS. He was excited and committed to learning how to be a successful leader but now saw that this was not a weekend project.

He had become comfortable with learning new software but realized that this wouldn't work like a new software program, where he could read the manual cover to cover and know how to use each feature. "Of course, this is why Grandfather chose the driving lessons as his example," Brian thought. "I didn't learn to drive in one weekend either." It was time to get dinner and a good night's sleep. Tomorrow was another opportunity to learn all he could at each step in the process.

PHASE ONE—RELATIONSHIP
The Relationship Built Through Leadership is Remembered Long After Understanding and Knowledge Are Imparted.

Step One: Where are you going?
You have to know where you're going. If you don't know where you're going, you will never know if you've arrived.

Step Two: What are the conditions?
The information you gather by looking, listening, and learning will be that on which you base all future steps to successful leadership.

CHAPTER FOUR

FIRST THINGS FIRST

"BEFORE YOU ATTEMPT TO SET THINGS RIGHT, MAKE SURE YOU SEE THINGS RIGHT."

Blaine Lee

Brian played guitar for the youth service at his church every Sunday. This Sunday, as he did every week, he met the entire youth team at seven thirty for breakfast.

This was their time to plan the morning. As they ate, they would finalize the list of songs to play and decide on activities for the high school students. They already knew what the Pastor's message would be; it was shared earlier in the week so the youth team could prepare songs and activities to reinforce the message. Sometimes they had to change songs at this last meeting because one of the team couldn't make it to the service. This also gave them the chance to encourage each other to do their best with the high school students.

They all had jobs during the week and outside pressures with finances, family, and friendships. But this volunteer team of eight people who loved to play music also knew that what they did on those Sunday mornings might be the only hope for some of the kids in the auditorium that day.

They went to the auditorium to check on the lights and sound. As he drove, Brian looked at his GPS and thought about what his grandfather said about leadership yesterday and his homework assignment. He laughed, the kind of laugh that comes out when you finally understand something that has been right in front of you all along. He said out loud, "Songs and activities to reinforce the message; that's the purpose of our youth service team."

He continued as if he were teaching this to someone who was in his car. "Lights and sound in the auditorium; those are the conditions around our youth service team that could have an impact on our performance. Talking about pressures the team is experiencing, adjusting to who is on the team that week—that's the condition of the team that we monitor all the time. Grandfather was right—leadership doesn't have to be difficult; it's seen everywhere."

The youth-service team had a great morning, full of energy. Brian arrived home ready to begin his research and look for information about the economy and the small business accounting software industry. If he could finish that today, on Monday he would make appointments to talk to Lloyd and Arthur and listen to their experiences.

He would retrieve the employee survey results from human resources and talk to his new team members to listen to their frustrations and ideas for improvements. He would visit the sales department to understand their views of his department and to gather the customer survey information. It was going to be a busy time. He wasn't sure how long it would take to get through all of those appointments, but he would start on Monday. For now, first things first: research.

LOOK FOR INFORMATION

Brian spent the afternoon on the Internet researching the economy and his industry. He needed to gather some clear thoughts about his team's purpose and the conditions in and around his team.

He was already fairly well versed on the national economy. It was a presidential election year and he wanted to be up-to-date on the facts; he and his friends were active voters. They felt a responsibility to voice their informed opinion by voting. The news reports said that the United States economy wasn't growing fast enough and they were now hearing more about the European economy and the impact it might have on the national recovery.

He knew that the stock market had rebounded from the recession lows three years before and, although volatile, appeared to be staying in that range. Many companies were generating increasing profits but sales were flat. Increases in profits are often driven by trimming costs where possible. Companies were just not hiring at a pace that would drive down unemployment levels.

Several of his classmates from college still had not found jobs. Regulations were increasing and compliance with these regulations required investment, which meant more expense.

Brian summarized the theme of the general economy in his notes: *Businesses must control costs. Any product that a company purchases must generate savings that are greater than the price of the product.*

Next, he turned to his industry. Who were his customers and what products were being offered today?

He searched the Small Business Administration website and found great information. There are about twenty-seven million small businesses in the United States in almost all industries. Most have fewer than twenty employees and 78 percent have no employees other than the owner. They employ 50 percent of the private-sector workforce. There is a significant amount of turnover in the industry as only 33 percent of small businesses last ten years or more. Over 50 percent of these companies start with less than $50,000 in capital, and most of that comes from personal or family savings.

There were many websites that reviewed small business accounting software. He read his competitors' materials to see how they were selling their product and he read customer reviews and technology reviews to obtain an independent assessment of these packages.

He discovered that the highest-rated software offered a complete package that can be used by a one-person start-up and a five-hundred-employee business that has its own accounting staff. Most of the software packages offered the standard capabilities to handle areas such as accounts payable, accounts receivable, general ledger, payroll, and online banking, among others. With a few exceptions, the price for each package was comparable.

The feature that was mentioned most was how each package accomplished these accounting needs. The look and feel of the interface was important. Was the package easy to learn and easy to use? Did the standard report package fill the most common requirements or was there a need for the users to create their own reports? Some of the larger software firms were now offering online packages for which small businesses pay a monthly fee to access one or more parts of the entire package. This was being sold as a simple solution for the mobile customer of any size.

Brian summarized the overview of small businesses: *Small businesses are the backbone of the economy. There is enormous opportunity to provide the right accounting software to help small businesses succeed. Competition is not based on features—those are must haves. Competition is based on ease of use.*

He felt prepared for his fact-finding meetings. He had looked for information that was already available and formed opinions on what he thought that information was telling him. He would invest his research time now in listening to those with experience, and learn what the employees, executives, and customers had to say about this business.

LISTEN FOR INFORMATION

Monday morning he arrived at the SBC parking lot and couldn't wait to walk through the front doors and start his day. Only two days ago, he'd sat in this same spot not knowing what he was going to do. Now he knew exactly what he would do: simply follow the path of successful leaders before him.

Today was Lloyd Henry's monthly rally, the last monthly rally before he retired. Brian would have to talk to him today. As he walked to his office he could see Lloyd down the hall shaking hands and wearing that great smile that he always seemed to have. He loved people, and people loved him. As the parade of congratulators passed by, Lloyd stopped and reached out his hand to Brian, who took the opportunity to thank Lloyd for all he had done for the company. This was his chance; Brian asked if he could spend thirty minutes with him one-on-one before the day was over to learn from his knowledge of the small business industry. Lloyd said, "Of course. I am honored to share from my many years of experience. How about right now? What would you like to know?"

Brian opened his briefcase and took out the notes from yesterday's research. He remembered his grandfather saying "It's amazing how lucky you can be when you are prepared." If he hadn't done the research yesterday, or taken good notes, or brought the notes with him today, he wouldn't have been able to take advantage of this opportunity.

Brian started the interview. "Lloyd, you started the small business division here at SBC. Why did you start it, and what do think of the industry now?"

Lloyd looked away for a moment to collect his thoughts, remembering what he was thinking years ago when he pitched his idea to start a small business division. "Software is a difficult business, competition is tough.

"You have to decide what kind of company you are going to be. Are you imitators or innovators? Do you imitate what is already selling and hope to get your piece of the pie; or do you innovate away from the crowd and toward what isn't yet being sold? Most companies chase the big guys, and they are satisfied with being one of many options.

"I chose new ideas. I chose to innovate and create products that no one else was selling. Look at what is out there. Challenge the status quo. Are there needs not being met? That is why I have new software ideas each month—there are always needs not being met. I spent my time in the field talking to customers and potential customers, asking them what they wanted, and then I brought it back. You can do the same thing. Find out what customers want that they aren't getting and provide it for them."

With that, the interview was over. Lloyd headed down the hall to his rally. Brian sat back down and thought about what he just heard. Lloyd had summarized his whole career in software development with one question: Are you an imitator or an innovator?

He wondered if that was the right question for his career. Grandfather had talked about successful leaders from history and how we could learn from their achievements. The first lesson he learned was that 80 percent of most problems have been solved before; the other 20 percent is taking the initiative to accept the solution given to you and implementing it.

But Grandfather also started quite a few new companies in several new industries. It seemed that the answer to Lloyd's question was: it depends.

Brian took out his notepad and wrote: *Imitation is preferred when you are following success. Innovation is preferred when you are defining success.*

Brian felt that he had confirmed what he thought of the small-business accounting software industry. SBC could imitate the success of other companies in providing the standard accounting capabilities and could innovate and define success in providing software that was easier to use.

After attending Lloyd's final rally meeting, it was time for the monthly budget meeting. This was Brian's second budget meeting since being promoted to manager of accounting software. He didn't remember much from the first meeting, which took place shortly after he was promoted, except that he thought at the time he would never understand all of those numbers.

Now he would attend the meeting with a purpose: he needed to understand the condition of his team. How was the small business division performing? How was the accounting group performing?

Arthur, now the new head of the small business division, kicked off the meeting reassuring the division's management team that he didn't plan to change anything. He said, "As you will see when we review the budget, everything is fine. Revenues are stable, profits are stable, and I don't intend to rock the boat. All of us in this room have been doing our jobs for years; we know what to do. Finally, before we go around the room to hear each group talk about its results, I want to share my motto for success, which I have used to guide my career to this point and which I intend to use as my guide going forward."

Arthur held up a piece of paper with bold letters on it. "We have been given a job to do," he read to the audience, "and we will do it just as it was written."

There was that motto again. Brian knew what to expect from Arthur in his new role. He liked to see things remain the same: "no boat-rocking," he had just announced to his managers.

Brian listened to the manager of each group say the same thing; revenues and profits are stable. He went back to his office and dug into his group's performance. He didn't just want to know that his revenue and profits were stable, he wanted to know why his revenue and profit were stable.

He spent the rest of the day poring over his team's financial reports from the last few years. He found one report that was not discussed in the budget meeting; the same-store sales report. This report talked about the revenue generated from the same customers each quarter. It was a good measure of the value their products brought to their customers. Were customers purchasing more products as they grew? Were customers purchasing training classes to teach their employees how to use your software? The information on this report said the answer to those questions was no.

Their core set of software products and their best customers made up only 20 percent of their revenue. The other 80 percent came from new customers and new products. He remembered the Pareto Principle from college business classes. This principle said that 80 percent of your business comes from 20 percent of your customers. SBC small-business accounting software, it turned out, was just the opposite. This couldn't be sustainable. The report showed that they were losing as many customers as they gained each quarter. Why was this happening?

Brian picked up the phone and scheduled a meeting for tomorrow morning with Dan, the small-business sales manager.

He drove home and thought about tomorrow's meeting. This would be the first time he met with Dan. He wanted to establish a good working relationship, but as the manager of the accounting group he needed to understand why they weren't maintaining their customers.

He and his grandfather were alike in many ways. One was their passion for wanting to maximize everything. They both saw so much potential in every person and every situation that they sometimes came across as critical. In the spirit of wanting to help everyone succeed, they offered their opinions freely.

Grandfather gave Brian a laminated card to carry in his wallet. He said, "Read it when you really feel that passion to maximize someone or something, before you offer your opinion."

The card contained the words of Blaine Lee, one of the founders of the Franklin Covey Leadership Center. It said, "Before you attempt to set things right, make sure you see things right." He resolved to listen to Dan first and maximize second.

They met at the cafeteria for breakfast on Tuesday morning. Brian wanted this meeting to be informal; asking questions about why they were losing customers could come across as challenging the sales department.

He started the conversation by saying, "I am excited to work with you and your team. I really only have one question. What can I do to help your team be successful?"

Dan put his fork down and said, "I have been at SBC since the beginning of the company. I helped build the small business division. I hired every salesperson on our team; they are like a family to me. You are the first person in software development to ask that question since I joined the small business division. You will have to forgive me if I am not prepared to give an answer."

Dan finished his last bite of scrambled eggs and then said, "I consider myself a good judge of character, and I think you honestly want to help, so I'm just going to tell you. Are you ready?"

Of course Brian was ready; he had his notepad out and had already written some notes about Dan and his tenure at SBC, something he didn't know before. "In the early days of SBC Technology we were a much smaller company. We all worked together to deliver the best software to our customers. Development, sales, and training; we all worked together. SBC had a motto 'We don't have products we sell to customers; we have customers we sell products to.'

"Our goals were based on growing our customer base and the number of repeat sales to our current customers. We generated good revenue and profit using that way of doing business.

"When Lloyd joined the company to start the small business division, that all changed. The division grew so fast that it needed its own sales force. I volunteered to take on the sales manager role. I thought we could make the small business division an extension of SBC. The same values, the same culture, the same strategy. But Lloyd had other ideas. He turned around our motto.

"Before we knew it, our focus turned to the products that we sold to customers. Our goals changed to the number of new products sold. We stopped paying attention to repeat sales. You went to the monthly rallies, Brian. We heard a new idea each month and had to start selling the idea before it was developed to attract new customers.

"We still generate good revenue and profit today, but we have disappointed customers. Our current customers feel abandoned as we spend our time finding new customers. Many of our new customers switch to our competitions' products almost as fast as they buy our new products because we usually don't deliver what we promised. The customers who stay with our new products can't figure out how to use the software, and our salespeople spend time teaching them instead of selling to someone else.

"You asked me what you can do to help my sales team be successful. I'll tell you. Return to the values, culture, and strategy that made SBC great. Return our focus to the customer. Return to working together. Help us deliver software that we are proud of while we generate good revenue and profits. Help us build a strong customer base that won't want to use any other product but ours."

Brian kept writing to capture all of Dan's comments. He finished his notes by writing the old SBC motto: *We don't have products we sell to customers, we have customers we sell products to.*

He looked up and said, "Thank you. What you said makes sense. I hope you don't mind me saying this, but it sounds so simple. Why hasn't anyone else seen this and taken some action?"

"Oh, everyone sees this at first," Dan quickly responded. "But your vision gets clouded when you see that the rewards go to those who generate the most sales by bringing in the most new customers with the most new products. Everyone lost sight of the customer base because we stopped talking about the customer base. We try to do what we can in sales to serve our customers. We try to answer their training questions, but we're not technical experts, your developers are. And your developers can't help with training; they're too busy developing the next product.

"You're a leader in this company now. The suite of accounting software that you manage is the most important product for SBC. You are in a position to make a difference." Dan stood up and said, "Thanks for having breakfast with me. I enjoyed talking with you. Now it's back to work."

Brian sat back and thought about all that Dan said. He had discovered his team's purpose at SBC: *Deliver small business accounting software that generates good revenue and profits, while fulfilling customers' needs.*

He had three more pieces of research to accomplish: read the customer surveys, read the employee surveys, and talk to his team. His view of the conditions in and around SBC small business accounting was becoming clearer.

Brian returned to his office. He had a full week of work ahead. His team was still responsible for getting all the new products completed on time, and he needed to review their progress. Arthur's weekly staff meeting was on Friday and he wanted to be prepared.

During his first month of meetings he had listened more than he had talked. Each week he reviewed the delivery schedule, and his team was on track to deliver as they always did. But he wanted to make better use of the time in the staff meetings. He gathered the customer and employee surveys for the last two years and put them in his briefcase. He could read them this week in the evenings at the gym while he used the elliptical machine. He would still listen more than he talked at the staff meeting; he had a lot to learn. But he hoped to hear answers to the questions he would ask his new peers about SBC and its future. He spent the rest of the week talking to each of his four lead programmers and twenty-five programmers.

LEARN FROM INFORMATION

"Boy, did that week go fast," Brian thought as he unpacked his briefcase on Friday morning at the office.

He had four hours to summarize his notes from the week and prepare for Arthur's staff meeting. First, he needed to make sense of the handwritten notes he made on each of the surveys he read. He had highlighted positives and negatives on each one. He transferred each one into a spreadsheet with two columns. He intended to graph the results to look for trends.

When he looked at his data, the trends were evident even without a graph. The positives column had only one entry with several tick marks next to it. After reading all the quarterly customer surveys for the last two years, the only positive comments that he found said: *Great tools with unique capabilities.* The negative column had several entries such as: *Late deliveries, too many errors, and hard to learn.*

Next he summarized his notes from the employee surveys and his discussions with his team. Grandfather was right, the comments were much more open on the survey results than in his one-on-one discussions, but the themes were easy to spot: *Confusing direction on product expectations, unrealistic delivery dates, assigning projects to programmers without expertise in that specific area.* Some of this rang especially true to him as a member of this group for the last three years.

Brian opened up a new document on his computer and began retyping all of his summary statements onto one page. He needed a clear overview of the conditions in and around his team for the staff meeting.

WHAT IS THE PURPOSE OF MY TEAM?

To deliver small-business accounting software that generates good revenue and profits, while fulfilling customer's needs.

WHAT ARE THE CONDITIONS IN AND AROUND MY TEAM?

How is the general economy? Businesses must control costs. Any product that a company purchases must generate savings that are greater than the price of the product.

How is the small-business industry? Small businesses are the backbone of the economy. There is enormous opportunity to provide the right accounting software to help small businesses succeed. Competition is not based on features—those are must haves. Competition is based on ease of use.

How is SBC competing in the industry? SBC is innovating and creating products that no one else is selling.

How should SBC compete in the industry? SBC should imitate when following success and innovate when defining success.

How is SBC approaching its customers? SBC is generating sales by bringing in the most new customers with the most new products.

How should SBC approach its customers? SBC should focus on providing its customers with products they need, not finding customers for the products they have.

What are customers saying about SBC? SBC has tools with unique capabilities, but there are late deliveries, too many errors, and the software is hard to learn.

What are employees saying about SBC? They are receiving confusing directions on product expectations, unrealistic delivery dates, and project assignments that are out of their area of expertise.

There were six managers on the team. In addition to the accounting software that Brian managed, the small business division produced software for customer relationship management, data security, human resources, and communication. Rounding out the management team was Dan who managed sales.

Arthur led the discussion with each of his managers; Brian was scheduled to be last. He listened to the other managers report that their development was on track. They would deliver the new software just as sales had directed. Dan gave the sales figures and reported that new customer acquisition was on schedule to drive the revenue numbers in the plan.

Brian looked at the clock and saw that he had ten minutes to present his group's report. He echoed what the others said about being on track with software delivery then heard the click of pens as they were closed and put back into pockets and he saw notebooks being closed. Everyone thought he was done with his report.

"Before you go, I have a couple of questions I would like to ask." He looked to Dan for encouragement and saw a smile that told him to keep going.

"I am new to this leadership role, I need your guidance on some information I have come across. Each week we all report our progress in developing new software and obtaining new customers. My research on the industry and SBC suggests that we are focusing on the wrong goal.

"The leading software producers have a broad suite of standard products that are rated highly for how easy they are to use for any size small-business customer. Our own customer research says that SBC's products are unique and deliver something that no one else in the industry delivers, but they are difficult to use and don't always work as promised."

The room was very quiet as his peers looked at Arthur for his reaction to what Brian had just said. Arthur cleared his throat, shuffled his papers and said, "You were right when you said you were new to your leadership role. Let me help you understand. Do you see those words behind me?" Arthur pointed to the poster on the wall, the same poster that had been in his office was now hanging in the board room. He read the words out loud, "We have been given a job to do, and we will do it just as it was written." With that, the meeting was over.

Brian was stunned. It all seemed so clear to him. His research on the economy, the industry, and the team all led to one answer; SBC had to change to survive. Brian closed his notebook, put his pen in his pocket, and walked back to his office. How could he change the company if they couldn't see what needed to be changed?

CHAPTER FIVE

HOW ARE YOU GOING TO GET TO YOUR DESTINATION?

GREAT LEADERS DON'T ROCK THE BOAT, THEY USE THE WAVES OF SUCCESS TO LIFT AND CARRY THEIR TEAM FORWARD.

It had been one week since Brian last heard his grandfather's voice on the GPS. In that time, he had taken the first two steps to becoming a great leader: purpose and conditions. That was his homework. Until yesterday afternoon, he thought he was on the right track, but wasn't sure now.

He and Dan had really connected, but his four other peers didn't seem the least bit interested in what he was saying at the staff meeting and his ideas were immediately rejected by Arthur. He took a morning run by the lake to clear his head and replay what Grandfather had said last Saturday: "Your homework assignment is to research and understand steps one and two about your leadership assignment."

Brian stopped and looked out at the lake and repeated those words over and over, "research and understand, research and understand, research and understand." He turned and started jogging home then stopped again and said, "Nowhere in my assignment did he say implement everything you have learned." That was it. That is why the staff meeting was such a disaster. He had done exactly what Arthur always said he would never do: rock the boat.

Looking out at the lake, he remembered the weekend he and his grandfather had spent at this very lake. They'd rented a small boat. It was a calm day, but the forecast called for wind. He remembered that he'd asked his grandfather why they were going out on the lake if it might get rough. In reply, his grandfather had said, "The one who stays on the shore because there might be waves will be the one who waves from the shore at the ship returning full of fish." At the beginning of the tour he hadn't known what that meant, but he knew he would find out by the end.

As they arrived at the dock, he noticed the waves. It was a calm day and in the distance he could see only a trace of movement in the water. As they approached their sailboat the man who rented the boat to them said, "Be careful as you step aboard; even tied to the dock on a calm day, the boats are rocking."

They started the small motor and steered the boat out of the dock. As they made their way through the lake, the boat rocked in the wake of the other boats. It took about an hour before they stopped at an area of the lake with no one else around.

Grandfather opened the cooler and brought out the sandwiches and drinks. They enjoyed the gentle sound of the waves and the feeling of the boat slowly rocking back and forth as they ate their lunch and talked. They didn't talk about anything in particular, just a bit of everything: baseball, school, books, and movies.

When Grandfather packed up the cooler, Brian asked if this was the end of their tour and his answer came when Grandfather pulled out two oars and said, "We still have a little farther to go and without a good wind the sails won't work."

The boat rocked as they rowed until the wind picked up. It was time to raise the sails and bring the boat back to the dock. With the wind blowing and the sails up, the boat rocked quite a bit as they sailed back to the marina.

On the drive home, Grandfather repeated what he'd said at the beginning of the day. "The one who stays on the shore because there might be waves, will be the one who waves from the shore at the ship returning full of fish." He used the boat tour to explain what he meant. "As long as we were in the boat, it was rocking. It didn't matter if we used the motor, the oars, or the sail to keep moving forward. You see, in life, just as in boating, you can't expect calm waters to move you forward toward success. The only time you don't feel the boat rocking is when you aren't in the boat; the faster you are moving forward, the more the boat rocks.

"If you want to make a difference in this world, if you want to be the captain of the boat that is bringing in the fish, you don't rock the boat; you use the waves of success to lift and carry you forward."

Brian realized that Arthur was right—a leader shouldn't rock the boat. If your team is moving forward, then the boat will already be rocking. If your team is not moving forward, then no amount of rocking will make the boat move forward.

STEP THREE: HOW ARE YOU GOING TO GET TO YOUR DESTINATION?

Brian finished his run and returned home. After he cleaned up, he sat down at his desk, turned on his laptop and the GPS, and was ready to learn step three. He typed SUCCESSFUL LEADERSHIP in the GPS and pressed GO. Once again Grandfather's familiar, calming voice came through. "Welcome back, Brian. I trust that you were successful in finding the purpose for your team and the conditions in and around your team.

"Before we begin step three, I want to tell you about Robert F. Kennedy, the younger brother of John F. Kennedy, the thirty-fifth president of the United States.

"He was the attorney general during the early 1960s and was instrumental in moving forward the cause of civil rights in the United States. He used US marshals to enforce the 1954 Supreme Court desegregation decision and admit the first African American student to the University of Mississippi. He hired the first African American lawyer to the Office for Civil Rights. Most importantly, he worked with President Kennedy and President Johnson to create the Civil Rights Act of 1964, a broad, important law to protect the civil rights of all US citizens without regard to race or gender.

"With all of these accomplishments to his credit, Kennedy said, 'Few will have the greatness to bend history itself, but each of us can work to change a small portion of events...it is from numberless acts of courage and belief that human history is shaped.' You see Brian, Robert F. Kennedy did change history, one act of courage at a time.

"I told you this story because just as the GPS knows where you are in your driving journey, I know where you are in your leadership journey. I have been there many times myself as have many leaders before. Where you are today is a strong desire to have an impact on everything you have learned in steps one and two. That is a desire you should not release, but fulfill.

"You will fulfill this desire through the remaining steps, proved time and again to bring success. The Chinese philosopher Lao Tzu, who lived in the sixth century BC, described the process that brings success: 'Water is fluid, soft, and yielding. But water will wear away rock, which is rigid and cannot yield. As a rule, whatever is fluid, soft, and yielding will overcome whatever is rigid and hard.' With that, we will now start your lesson on the third step in phase one of leadership."

Brian stopped the GPS to catch up with notes he needed to take. He had been so engrossed in Grandfather's story that he just listened. He listened to Grandfather's words and to the increasing beat of his heart. He realized that he was learning the steps that would change lives forever. Then he once again typed SUCCESSFUL LEADERSHIP in the GPS, pressed GO, and picked up where he left off.

"Step three in your driving lesson was determining how you were going to get to the destination you chose in step one, while considering the conditions in and around your car that you discovered in step two.

"If you were going to the mall by yourself on a clear, warm day and your car had just been tuned up, then you could get in and go. You could take any number of local streets. You really didn't need to plan your route; you could decide on the way depending on traffic conditions. For other journeys that would take longer, with other people in the car and with more potential for poor weather, you needed to be more diligent in planning.

"We talked about the long vacation car trips to the beach that your grandmother and I joined you on when you were young. There was a lot of planning. The GPS systems that are common place now weren't in use then. Your father and I reviewed paper maps and highlighted the route we wanted to take. We considered the weather and the type of roads to take. We planned to drive on highways, where possible, that would be clear of snow and have restaurants and hotels nearby so we could stop to eat and sleep each night. Our role was to ensure that we arrived at the destination safely, well rested, on time, and ready to enjoy our vacation.

"When I taught you how to drive, I ended the story there. I didn't tell you how your mother and grandmother had different roles in planning the trip. Their role was very important then and will be very important for you in your leadership assignment.

"They researched and planned activities for us to do while we were on vacation. They gathered brochures and books about our destination that showed pictures of the hotel we would call home for two weeks. They highlighted interesting and educational sights we could visit along our planned route. I remember the excitement during the days leading up to the vacation trips.

"Those days were just as important as the two weeks we would spend together at the beach. For a week prior to the trip, your parents would show you and your sister, Karen, the pictures of the hotel, the beach, the bikes you would ride, and the boat you would rent for little day trips. And each night, they would reveal one of the sights you would visit on your route to the beach and on your route home."

As a child, Brian had no idea this much planning was needed for what seemed to him to be a simple car trip to the beach. But he remembered how he and Karen would anticipate the fun they were going to have on the car trip to the beach, being at the beach, and on the car trip back home.

"Too many times, vacations can be difficult. Being cooped up in a car for days, a small hotel room for days, then a car again for days can wear on anyone's patience. Those days of building up the fun and excitement helped everyone enjoy the entire trip. Every day in the car seemed shorter with the planned stops along the route. Every night in the hotel room seemed like an adventure as we talked about the next day's fun yet to come.

"Your leadership journeys will be much more like the long family vacation trips than a quick drive to the mall. Our family vacation trips were fun one day at a time because we made them fun for each family member. You will be successful in achieving the purpose for your team one day at a time by helping each team member achieve success. Our family vacation trips were the culmination of many small trips. Achieving your team's purpose will be the culmination of many small achievements."

Brian remembered their family vacation car trips very well—how much fun the entire trip was; not just the two weeks at the beach, but the drive there and the drive home. He and his sister played the "I can't wait" game in the back row of their minivan. Each of them took turns trying to top the other as they said, "I can't wait until we get to the next destination. I am going to..." then fill in the rest with something fun.

He looked at the clock; it was 10:00 a.m. He was meeting his mom and dad for lunch at one. He wanted to tell them about the GPS and all he was learning from Grandfather. He wanted to tell them how his life as a leader was being changed every day. Maybe it was all the thoughts about his childhood and hearing his grandfather's voice again that made him call his mom on Wednesday and schedule this lunch.

He didn't always see eye to eye with his parents. "Your life begins with your family, and it ends with your family," Grandfather would say to his children and grandchildren. "You may not be feeling connected right now, but you are connected nonetheless.

"Always remember that your journey in life may take you in different directions. But the road home is always clear and ready for travel; and at the end of the road home are open arms."

Brian had two more hours of leadership lessons before he headed to his parent's home for lunch.

"Step three in leadership is the same as in driving; determining how you are going to get to the destination you decided on in step one; while considering the conditions in and around your team that you discovered in step two.

"In leadership, your vision sets the route your team will take to reach its purpose. Our vision for driving to the beach for the family vacation was not complicated; similarly your vision for leading your team must be uncomplicated.

"Colin Powell, the retired US four-star general and former secretary of state, said, 'Great leaders are almost always great simplifiers, who… offer a solution everybody can understand.' We talked each day about our plans for our family vacation so you and Karen would stay focused on the fun we were going to have and not the long drive.

"Once you establish your vision, you must repeat it to maintain focus. Theodore Hesburgh was the President of Notre Dame for thirty-five years, the longest running president in the university's history. During his presidency, enrollment and awarded degrees doubled, the number of faculty doubled, and the endowment funds rose to $350 million. During his time at Notre Dame, Hesburgh also served on the US Civil Rights Commission, a science commission established by Dwight Eisenhower, and an immigration reform commission established by Jimmy Carter. This successful leader said, 'The very essence of leadership is that you have a vision. It's got to be a vision you articulate clearly and forcefully on every occasion. You can't blow an uncertain trumpet.'

"I think it would help at this point to give you an example of a simple, easy-to-understand vision of leadership in practice. Tony Dungy was the head coach for the Tampa Bay Buccaneers and the Indianapolis Colts. During his tenures, the Buccaneers won the NFC Central Division Championship, and the Colts won the Super Bowl. The purpose of each of his teams was to win games while having a positive influence on the community around them. Dungy knew the conditions in and around each of his teams. While they were different teams with different conditions, his vision for achieving their purpose was the same: 'Do the ordinary things better than anyone else; do whatever it takes to achieve excellence, no excuses, no explanations.'

"Dungy chose five areas of ordinary things for his team to focus on doing better than anyone else: top five in the NFL in giveaway/takeaway ratio, top five in the NFL in fewest penalties, top five in overall special teams, make big plays, and don't give up big plays.

"The final advice I will give you on step three comes from Vaclav Havel. He was the last president of Czechoslovakia, and the first president of the Czech Republic. He said, 'Vision is not enough. It must be combined with venture. It is not enough to stare up the steps; we must step up the stairs.'

"For your vision to be effective you have to set it in motion. I call this quick wins. On our family vacation car trips, our quick wins were activities such as making sure all the suitcases fit in the car, filling the cooler with drinks and snacks, and loading a variety of CDs in the player. These are actions that move you closer to starting the route that will lead you to your destination.

"For quick wins to be effective they must support your vision and have an immediate impact on your team. Your team needs to feel that their job satisfaction is improving. Remember that in phase one you are establishing trust. Your team is not yet ready to follow your leadership, so these quick wins need to be events that you can personally influence.

ASSIGNMENT

"Brian, your next assignment is to develop a vision that will achieve your team's purpose considering the conditions in and around your team, and select some quick wins to establish trust in your vision.

"Take your time. Think carefully about the words you use and the order in which they are used. Your team must understand what they will accomplish and how they will accomplish it.

"Once you complete this assignment, come back to the GPS. There is one more step for you to learn before you begin to implement your quick wins."

Brian turned off the GPS and summarized what he just learned. *Successfully achieving your team's purpose comes through a vision that consistently delivers many small successes for each team member.* He turned off his laptop and headed out to spend some time with his family.

Brian was always close with his parents even if they didn't agree on everything. His life had been so busy after college that they didn't see each other much other than the holidays. His mother was especially pleased to hear how her father had recorded his teaching so Brian could continue to be mentored. That was a fitting tribute to her father's life which was dedicated to helping others succeed. She told Brian that his grandfather would be happy that he made their family connection strong again.

This Sunday, after the usual meeting with the youth service team for breakfast, the service was tremendous. The youth band was better than he had ever heard. These Sunday breaks gave him a chance to release the pressure of the week and reflect on how he and his friends could have an impact on the youth of the area. He had already started thinking of introducing the idea of leadership lessons for the teenagers in his church, but he didn't feel like he was prepared for that just yet. Maybe when he had a few of the steps of successful leadership under his belt and saw the impact at SBC, he would be more comfortable bringing that up with his youth team.

Brian did his best thinking outside, so he took an afternoon bicycle ride by the lake. He reviewed all he had learned so far. His team's purpose was to deliver small-business accounting software that generated good revenue and profits, while fulfilling customers' needs. They were generating revenue and profit today, but it didn't seem sustainable. Their customers were spending too much time trying to learn how to use the SBC software instead of selling their own products or services. The employees had no control over their success or the success of SBC due to the lack of prioritization and project management. He could only change what he controlled: his team. But he had to do it in a way that continued to deliver the revenue and profits.

When he returned home he sat back down at his laptop and typed. He typed all the ideas he had while he was riding his bike. Some of his ideas sounded great in his head, but on paper they made no sense. He kept working until late.

After writing, deleting, changing, and spell-checking, he came up with what he thought was the solution to his team's vision and quick wins. The SBC small-business accounting software group needed to be experts in delivering what the customers wanted.

He would need to establish several new processes to help them become experts. He created a one-page vision and quick-win statement to hand out in meetings. He planned on sharing his vision 'clearly and forcefully on every occasion' just as Theodore Hesburgh said a leader should do. He turned off his laptop. Tomorrow evening after work he would return to the GPS for his next lesson.

SBC Small Business Accounting
Software Group Vision

We will fulfill our customers' small-business accounting needs by delivering software that we are proud to put the SBC name on: **S**imple to use, **B**y the promised due date, and **C**omprehensive.

We will deliver solutions to our customers' accounting needs by being:

- Expert listeners and learners so we understand our customer's needs.
- Expert organizers so we focus on the right priorities.
- Expert programmers so we develop the simplest solution possible.
- Expert project managers so we deliver error free and on time.

SBC Small-Business Accounting
oftware Group Quick Wins

We will implement the following initiatives to put us on the path to achieve our vision:

- Establish a partnership with sales to develop an understanding of our customers' needs and a process to jointly discuss solutions.
- Establish a product and sales prioritization committee to jointly set and track product deliveries.
- Establish a process to assign the right programmer with the right skill set to the right piece of the product development project.
- Establish a training program to ensure that our programmers have the skills needed to deliver the products needed.
- Establish a process to ensure that all software is certified as error free before delivery.

PHASE ONE—RELATIONSHIP
The Relationship Built Through Leadership Is Remembered Long After Understanding and Knowledge Are Imparted.

Step One: Where are you going?
You have to know where you're going. If you don't know where you're going, you will never know if you've arrived.

Step Two: What are the conditions?
The information you gather by looking, listening, and learning will be that on which you base all future steps to successful leadership.

Step Three: How are you going to get to your destination?
Successfully achieving your team's purpose comes through a vision that consistently delivers small successes for each team member.

CHAPTER SIX

BE PREPARED FOR DETOURS

TO SUCCEED IN REACHING YOUR DESTINATION, EXPECT DETOURS AND HAVE A PLAN TO WORK AROUND OR THROUGH THEM.

Brian thought about his vision and quick wins all day at work on Monday. He thought about the conditions he had discovered and how he could help his team and SBC be more successful.

He held back from trying to implement his vision and quick wins; he'd learned his lesson last week. Instead he wrote a note to himself each time he felt the urge to tell someone. He was sure he was on the right track. He had a page full of notes from Monday's meetings where he saw that his vision and quick wins were the answer to his team's problems.

He arrived home ready to eat and learn the step that Grandfather said he needed before he could begin to implement his vision. He sat down at his desk, turned on his laptop and GPS, typed in SUCCESSFUL LEADERSHIP and pressed GO.

STEP FOUR: BE PREPARED FOR DETOURS

"Hello, Brian," Grandfather started. "I know you are ready to start implementing all you learned in steps one and two with the vision and quick wins you developed in step three. So let's get right into step four of phase one.

"At this point in your driving lessons, you learned that you need to select a destination, examine the conditions in and around your car, and decide what route you will take. Before we backed the car out of the driveway you learned step four; be prepared for detours.

"When we set our route, we assume that nothing will interrupt our journey. New drivers haven't experienced the detours that may cause them to veer off their route. To succeed in reaching your destination, expect detours and have a plan to move around or through them. If a road is closed for construction, you'll need a map or a GPS to find a way around it and back to your route. Keep a safe distance between you and the car in front of you and pay attention to brake lights in case traffic suddenly slows down or stops.

"As a leader you will also experience detours that may cause you to veer off your vision unless you have plans to move around them or through them.

"Detours that keep you from driving on your chosen route are physical impediments such as construction trucks, emergency vehicles, or damaged cars. The detours you will face as a leader are not physical impediments, but the responses of some of the people around you whose lives are being changed. In both driving and leading, if you pay attention you will see the detours coming and be able to take action to avoid running into them or being stopped by them.

"The reason some people respond negatively to a life-changing vision is that they are human. Dr. James Belasco, founder of the San Diego University's Management Development Center and author of several bestselling books, has consulted businesses on leadership for over twenty years. In his book *Flight of the Buffalo* he said, 'Change is hard because people overestimate the value of what they have—and underestimate the value of what they may gain by giving that up.' Large changes, like moving from where your team is now to where your vision will take them, require giving up a lot. That is why you developed quick wins. These are the small successes that will lead your team to your vision, giving up a little each time. Remain calm when people challenge your vision. Recognize that it isn't personal, it is a natural response to change."

Brian understood now why Grandfather wanted him to learn this step before trying to implement his vision. Now he wouldn't be surprised to be challenged, but would expect it and have a plan to keep moving forward.

"In my research on great leaders, I found examples in all walks of life. A pattern emerged no matter the industry, the time in history, or the location. There are four responses that emerge in an attempt to stop or slow down change. Your particular plan for continued success will differ slightly for each of these four responses but your theme will remain the same: focus on your vision. Automobile industry pioneer Henry Ford had this same idea in mind when he said 'Obstacles are those frightful things you see when you take your eyes off your goal.'

"The first response to change is *fear of failure*. In this response, there will be doubt cast over the possibility that your vision will work. Comments will be made about your vision and your ability to deliver your vision. You can recognize this response by comments such as 'This has been tried before and it didn't work,' or 'He has never led a group this large, I am not sure he can do this.' When this response occurs, don't spend your time debating when comments are made; instead invest your time achieving your quick wins, one at a time. There is no better way to remove doubt or fear than through the observation of success.

"The second response to change is *forced failure*. In this response, there will be action taken to impede any progress on your vision and derail the train of success you have set in motion. This response can come in the form of intentionally missed or incorrectly completed assignments. You may also see that one or more people will refuse to agree on the next steps, but instead will want to debate the solution endlessly. Your action to prevent this response from stopping your vision must be quick, calm, and confident. Take each person responding in this way aside and discuss their response one-on-one. Acknowledge and validate their fear of the change that is occurring, and reassure them that your vision will create success for everyone, including them. Finish the conversation by reaffirming your commitment to your vision with a promise to not let their actions interfere with the success of the rest of the team. Once your team knows that you are committed to their success, they will commit to your vision.

"The third response to change is *false friendship*. In this response, your attention will be drawn to other activities in an attempt to take the focus away from your vision. Statements that start with 'Let me tell you as a friend' or 'No one can do this as you can' are frequently meant to divert your efforts to areas away from your vision. Your time is limited and should be invested in achieving the purpose and vision of your team. If the suggestion or request does not bring you closer to success, return your focus to your vision and proceed. Don't let flattery cause you to forget your focus.

"The fourth and final response to change is *false facts*. In this response, your intentions will be challenged through statements that misrepresent the truth in order to convince others not to follow your vision. For your vision to be successful, your team must believe in your intentions. Your team will turn to you for an answer to these claims. Do not argue or spend time trying to prevent these challenges from occurring. Instead admonish the challenger and demonstrate your intentions by recounting the success of the team and moving forward to further success. The proof of your character comes through in the lives of those on whom you have an impact." Brian summarized the four responses to change that he could expect to face—the detours, as Grandfather called them.

DETOURS ON THE ROAD TO SUCCESS AND THE PLAN TO WORK AROUND OR THROUGH THE DETOURS

FEAR OF FAILURE
Achieve quick wins to demonstrate the vision.
There is no better way to remove doubt or fear than through the observation of success.

FORCED FAILURE
Acknowledge and reaffirm your commitment to the vision.
Once your team knows that you are committed to their success, they will commit to your vision.

FALSE FRIENDSHIP
Analyze intentions and return your focus to the vision.
Don't let flattery cause you to forget your focus.

FALSE FACTS
Admonish detractors and proceed with your vision.
The proof of your character comes through in the lives of those on whom you have an impact.

ASSIGNMENT
"Now with the lessons of steps one through four completed, you are prepared to implement your quick wins.

"You will experience the most detours in the beginning of your leadership journey as you introduce your vision, but remember this lesson throughout your career. Detours can and do happen at any point on the journey.

"You will start to see the beginnings of success in your leadership journey. While you will face some detours, you will also see the lives of your team begin to change, and they will too. This is an exciting time for everyone involved, and it will all be accomplished with the first four of the five steps of phase one of leadership.

"In our family vacations, we had not yet started our trip. We knew the destination, the conditions we would travel through, and the route we would take. Now we were about to load the car with suitcases, snacks, and music. You are at the same point in your leadership journey; close to finalizing your preparation.

"Step five is the final step that you will take to complete your preparation. We will cover step five when you have invested enough time to see all the positive results that will come from what you have learned." Brian turned off his laptop and the GPS. He was ready to announce his vision and quick wins when he returned to work tomorrow.

IMPLEMENTING THE QUICK WINS

Brian met first with Dan. He thought he would be supportive of his ideas because he wanted SBC to change; he wanted SBC to be successful. They talked for a couple of hours as Brian shared what he learned about SBC through his research, discussions, and reading surveys. He laid out what he thought was the purpose for SBC and his vision for achieving that purpose. Dan responded energetically, "It seems like old times. You are describing the SBC that I knew and loved. I am going to ask you a question that a very wise person once asked me. What can I do to help your team be successful?" Brian remembered asking that same question of Dan when they first met. Now he was the wise one. He answered the question by showing him his list of five quick wins. He pointed out that for the first two quick wins to work, he needed Dan's support. The other three were up to him and his team.

- Establish a partnership with sales to develop an understanding of our customer's needs and a process to jointly discuss solutions.
- Establish a product and sales prioritization committee to jointly set and track product deliveries.
- Establish a process to assign the right programmer with the right skill set to the right piece of the product development project.
- Establish a training program to ensure that our programmers have the skills needed to deliver the products needed.
- Establish a process to ensure that all software is certified as error free before delivery.

Dan said, "Of course I support your quick wins. These are great ways to return our focus to the customer and to working together again. But remember our monthly budget meetings and how you defined the purpose of SBC; generate revenue and profit. You have to find a way to move in the direction of your quick wins while still delivering the products, revenue, and profit."

They talked some more and decided that it would take time to develop the level of customer research and product planning that SBC needed to design new products from a different perspective.

There were three products in the process of being developed that could fit into the five quick wins where they stood. There was one product that was near the delivery date, one in the middle of development, and one that sales had just committed to but had not yet been fully designed. All three could be tracked through the new product and sales prioritization committee. The product near the delivery date could go through the new certification process. Brian could make sure the right programmer was assigned to the right piece of the product in development. They both could bring together sales and development to discuss the right solution for the newest product. This would give them the chance to demonstrate that they could be successful delivering software that was easy to use, on time and without errors.

When these three current products were successfully launched, they would be able to extend their quick wins into more customer research and product design up front. For now Brian would work to develop his team's trust as Grandfather taught him was so important.

He and Dan scheduled a meeting for the following Monday with his entire team of developers and the sales force. He needed the time to prepare his presentation.

Brian was comfortable giving presentations. He enjoyed having a chance to communicate with people and he liked the challenge of connecting with people. In the last two years of college he and his classmates worked in teams. Every project was graded at a team level. The team grade came from the presentation of their work, in which they discussed how they worked together on the project and the results. Each team graded every other team equally on four items: team participation, collaboration, clarity of results, and the success of the project. In time, it became evident that a team with the best results could still get the lowest grade if they didn't work together well, or if they didn't communicate their results well.

"If you fail to prepare you are preparing to fail," Grandfather would say, quoting John Wooden, the former head basketball coach at UCLA, and one of his favorite leaders. Brian worked hard over the next week preparing for his presentation. He studied the product launches of Apple and how Steve Jobs held the audience in anticipation, one simple message at a time. He studied a quote from Steve Jobs he came across that said, "That's been one of my mantras—focus and simplicity. Simple can be harder than complex. You have to work hard to get your thinking clean to make it simple. But it's worth it in the end because once you get there, you can move mountains." Jobs didn't talk about what Apple wasn't, but what it was and what it would be.

Brian was part of the audience when Apple product launches occurred; he watched live via the Internet. He remembered feeling excited, energized, and ready to conquer the world with the latest Apple product. He wanted to deliver that feeling to his audience; he wanted to move mountains.

He remembered a quote from Michelangelo he'd heard while on his ninth grade trip to Europe with his grandfather. "A great statue already exists inside a block of stone. The sculptor's role is to uncover it." SBC was a good company that had greatness within it. He determined that his message would be simple and forward looking. He would focus on his vision and what SBC would become.

THE PRESENTATION

On the following Monday Brian arrived at the SBC office early. Today's meeting with his team and the sales team was important. This was the first time he would address them all as a group. For SBC to be successful, this group had to work together to accomplish a shared vision. "You never get a second chance to make a first impression," he remembered Grandfather saying.

He checked the lights and air conditioning in the meeting room. He remembered from college lectures how distracting it was when it was too hot or cold, or the lights were too bright or dim. He tested the remote for his presentation; there was no room for technical problems to take the focus off his simple message.

Brian delivered his presentation. He shared his vision for the SBC small-business accounting software group.

The first slide had one simple message.
SBC SMALL BUSINESS ACCOUNTING SOFTWARE IS:
SIMPLE TO USE
BY THE PROMISED DUE DATE
COMPREHENSIVE

The second slide had one word
EXPERTS

The next four slides each contained only a few words:
EXPERT LISTENERS AND LEARNERS
EXPERT ORGANIZERS
EXPERT PROGRAMMERS
EXPERT PROJECT MANAGERS

As each slide was on the screen, Brian talked about SBC as if he was describing how it operated today, not what it might be someday. Next he talked about the five initiatives they would implement to further enhance SBC's expert status. One initiative was shown on each of the next five slides.

PARTNER WITH SALES TO DEVELOP SOLUTIONS

PARTNER WITH SALES TO PRIORITIZE PROJECTS

MATCH PROGRAMMER SKILLS TO PROJECT NEEDS

TRAIN PROGRAMMERS IN NEEDED SKILLS

DELIVER ERROR-FREE SOFTWARE

Brian finished his presentation and asked if there were any questions. A few members of both his team and the sales team asked to go back and talk in more detail about how this would work in practice. "How are sales and development going to partner? Will we go on sales calls together?" One of the programmers asked when she could begin training classes on the latest development tools. He let the teams brainstorm for a while. He could see the stone being chiseled away, revealing the beginning of the masterpiece of SBC.

Then it happened, just as Grandfather said it would. Tom, a programmer who recently started at SBC, stood up and asked to speak. "I came to SBC six months ago. I joined because of SBC's reputation for always being on the leading edge, always developing the latest software. The last two companies I worked for were small. They tried to change but couldn't compete and I lost my job. What I heard today suggests a radical change from what made SBC successful. What if it doesn't work? I don't want to be out of work again."

Every eye turned from Tom to Brian. As he stepped to the front of the room, he was grateful for Grandfather's lesson on detours. He didn't see this detour coming so soon, it was his first, but he was prepared to handle the fear-of-failure response to change—focus on achieving your quick wins since there is no better way to remove doubt or fear than through the observation of success.

Brian took the microphone. "When I was in high school I wanted to be on the track team. I trained all summer to get ready. When school started I procrastinated in signing up for tryouts. One day my grandfather asked me if I made the team. I told him I was too afraid to try out. 'What if I'm not good enough?' I asked him.

"He said, 'The only real failure in life is the failure to try. The greatest football quarterbacks complete only six of ten passes. The best basketball players make only half of their shots. In baseball if you can get a hit more than three out of ten times at bat you'll be in the hall of fame. Just like all of these sports stars, you are guaranteed to finish last if you never get up to the line of scrimmage, or on the court, or in the batter's box. To get a chance to win, you have to take the chance to lose.

"You have Dan's and my commitment. SBC small-business accounting software will be the best it can be. We are going to start by focusing on the three products that are in the development process now. We will deliver what we promised, only better. There is one product that's near delivery. We can't make a lot of changes to its functionality, but we can focus on testing to make sure it has no defects. Shipping is sixty days away. If the product isn't perfect, we will learn from what worked and what didn't work and be even better the next time. Recognize that we will get closer to our destination each time by moving forward and not by standing still."

He ended the meeting and began implementing the quick wins. The prioritization and project tracking committee was started and a new testing program was implemented. Sixty days later the most recent product reached the market with significantly fewer errors than previous software releases. The customer response was very positive, and the employee response was even better. Brian celebrated the success of this first change at their next quarterly all-staff meeting.

With success on this quick win, the talk about fearing failure had ended. They proceeded to implement the remaining quick wins using the two other products in development as testing grounds. Brian reviewed the programmer assignments for the second product and reassigned some of the work to match up skills with needs. Next he worked with SBC's head of HR and training to set up a training curriculum and certification system for his programmers to qualify for different levels of product development. Lastly, Brian and Dan selected representatives from their teams to begin the customer-needs and solution-development group.

Over the next thirty days, the teams made great progress. The solution development group came up with some great ideas for how the newest product could deliver what the customer really needed.

After aligning programmers' skills to the right pieces of the project, the second product was ahead of schedule and the morale was higher. There was a buzz in the office that hadn't existed before. Programmers asked questions and exchanged ideas to help one another be successful. While reviewing the project reports, Brian noticed that one of the programmers, Jacob, was falling behind and the rest of the team was making up for his mistakes. Brian was happy to see the team come together to keep the project on track, but he was concerned that Jacob was making mistakes.

They had worked together for the last three years at SBC. Jacob was one of the best programmers that Brian knew. As a matter of fact, he was in the running for the manager job that Brian was promoted to. Jacob's mistakes fit the signs of forced failure. Grandfather said that in order to maintain the commitment of the team, you have to acknowledge and validate the fear of change, but reaffirm your commitment to your vision. Brian invited Jacob to a working lunch in his office.

They talked about the success of the first product launch and Brian pointed out that they were ahead of schedule on the second product. Brian said, "The success of this team is not just the successful launch of products. It is also the individual success of each team member. I want you to be successful. I know you are more than capable of completing your assignments, and I understand that change is difficult and we are going through quite a bit of change. Let me tell you a story I learned about commitment to excellence.

"When I was in the high school orchestra, we took a field trip to hear the professional symphony orchestra practice. After the session, the conductor talked about what it takes to succeed in a professional orchestra. He said, 'A chain is only as strong as its weakest link, and an orchestra is only as strong as its weakest player.

'Each piece of orchestra music is written for a specific number of musicians. Beethoven's fifth symphony was written to be played by fourteen musicians other than the string players: two flutes, two oboes, two clarinets, two bassoons, one contrabassoon, two French horns, two trumpets, and one timpani. There are roughly fifty professional orchestras in the United States. Since each one of these orchestras employs about fifty musicians, there are two thousand five hundred professional orchestra jobs across the United States. That sounds like a lot of jobs, until you compare that to the one hundred eighty thousand registered musicians in the United States.

'Being one of the top musicians is the price of entry to a professional orchestra. What really sets apart those musicians who last is their attitude and commitment to the excellence of the entire orchestra. Each musician must play the part written for their instrument, just as it was written. If each musician does this, we create beautiful music. If any musician sets themselves above the music, the entire symphony fails. As the conductor, I can't let that happen. Any musician who is not committed to the success of the entire orchestra will soon be replaced with one who is.'"

Jacob said he understood and thanked Brian for lunch. Over the next three months he did get back on track and helped the team deliver the second product on time, with no errors, and with an interface that was easier for the customer to use. They celebrated the success of the second product in their third quarterly all-staff meeting.

Brian reported on his team's progress in Arthur's staff meetings each Friday. He was excited about his team's success and it showed in his updates.

He made sure to point out that they were still delivering exactly what they promised, only better. Arthur was impressed with the progress Brian had made in such a short amount of time.

After the most recent meeting, one of the other managers, Chuck, rode the elevator with him. "I like your enthusiasm," Chuck said, "Let me help you as a friend. I hope all of your success continues. But over the long run, you won't get sales to cooperate. They always end up demanding more than you can deliver, then blaming the developers when it doesn't work. You need a back-up plan when this fails. You have to deliver what you are asked to deliver and generate sales. I wouldn't want to be in your shoes when this falls apart."

Brian's Grandfather had said, "A true friend doesn't just warn you about a stone in your path that may cause you to fall, they do their best to keep you from falling, and if that is not possible they are there to help you back up." Chuck's advice sounded like false friendship. Brian took Grandfather's counsel and continued to focus on his vision.

Seven months into implementing the quick wins, the third product was rolled out. This product had the advantage of being part of each quick win and the results were tremendous. It was delivered on time, error free, easy to use, and it fit the needs of the customer better than any product the SBC small-business accounting group ever delivered.

Brian and Dan held the fourth quarterly all-staff meeting for both of their teams. They celebrated the continued success of each product roll out.

After the meeting, Dan held up the latest customer surveys and said, "These ratings are off the charts. This is better than we ever did in the old SBC. I have to hand it to you, you did it." Brian shook Dan's hand and said, "No, we did it, development and sales together, with a focus on the customer."

They both turned to see Ron, SBC's top salesperson, walk by. "What was that?" Ron said. "Development and sales did this together? I don't think so. I am sales and I had no part of this. These last three products were the hardest to sell of any products we ever sold. You have no idea how much I had to smooth things over with our customers. If we keep up this way, I won't be able to cover for you in the field much longer. When my sales start to fall, I will make sure that Arthur hears it was your idea."

Brian recognized this response to change as false facts. He proceeded to recount their successes saying, "Let me see those surveys again. 'Best software I ever purchased; easiest implementation I ever experienced; if you keep this up I will never use anything other than SBC software.' Those don't sound too bad to me.

"Ron, I am sure you have heard of Albert Einstein and his many discoveries in modern science. When I was in college I learned that he discovered all he did in the pursuit of truth. He is quoted as saying, 'The right to search for the truth implies also a duty; one must not conceal any part of what one has recognized to be the truth.' And he also said, 'Whoever is careless with the truth in small matters cannot be trusted with important matters.'

"I have not hidden my plans from anyone. In fact Dan and I agreed on everything and Arthur has full knowledge of our plans. I have given updates to Arthur and his entire management team this whole year. You aren't being asked to sell more complicated products; they are easier. You aren't being asked to explain extended delivery times, they are faster. You aren't being asked to correct bugs; the new software is error free. You do have to change your sales style because you can now be proud of the products you are selling, and that is a good place to be."

Ron didn't offer his heartfelt agreement, but understood that he couldn't blame Brian or his vision for his sales performance. "All right, I will give this some time and see how it goes," Ron said as he left the room.

On the drive home Brian reflected on the three new product roll outs. It had all worked. The destination, conditions, vision, and quick wins worked together to create success. Brian had experienced the four responses to change and was prepared to move through or around them. It had been seven months since his last lesson.

He reached over to his GPS and typed in SUCCESSFUL LEADERSHIP and pressed GO. But there was no response. Brian knew Grandfather wouldn't stop teaching the leadership lessons now after only the first four steps. The last thing Grandfather said was, "We will cover step five when you have invested enough time to see all the positive results that will come from what you have learned."

He didn't know what else he could accomplish with what he had learned so far. Maybe more responses to change were coming as SBC's next product was developed. Brian trusted that Grandfather knew what he was doing. No need for him to worry about what was next. The weekend was here and Monday would come soon enough.

PHASE ONE—RELATIONSHIP
The Relationship Built Through Leadership Is Remembered Long After Understanding and Knowledge Are Imparted.

Step One: Where are you going?

You have to know where you're going. If you don't know where you're going, you will never know if you've arrived.

Step Two: What are the conditions?

The information you gather by looking, listening, and learning, will be that on which you base all future steps to successful leadership.

Step Three: How are you going to get to your destination?

Successfully achieving your team's purpose comes through a vision that consistently delivers small successes for each team member.

Step Four: Be prepared for detours

To succeed in reaching your destination, expect detours and have a plan to work around or through them.

CHAPTER SEVEN

MAKE ROOM FOR OTHERS

THE SUCCESS OF A JOURNEY OFTEN DEPENDS MORE ON WHO YOU ARE WITH THAN WHERE YOU ARE GOING.

Brian arrived home to the blinking of his answering machine. There were three messages waiting for him.

The first was from Joseph, one of his best friends from college. "It's that time of year again—the Memorial Day weekend bicycle tour. We're going to the California Sierra." The second was from Elliot, another friend from college. "Ten-thousand-foot climbs, views like the Alps. We're all going. It won't be the same without you." The third message was from Sam, the last of the group from college. "We all committed to stay connected. You have to come on our annual bike trip."

It wasn't like his friends to call his home phone and leave messages. They e-mailed, sent texts, and posted on Facebook; worst case, they would talk on their smart phones. Brian hadn't been keeping up with his friends lately. The last seven months took a lot of his time. Vision, quick wins, detours; he was responsible for all of it. He hadn't even thought of their annual Memorial Day weekend bike tour.

Brian and his three friends were inseparable in college. They didn't have the same courses; Joseph majored in finance, Elliot in marketing, Sam in pre-law, and Brian in computer science. But wherever you saw one, another was close by; they supported each other. They were each unique in their skills and abilities but the same when it came to offering a hand to a friend.

They made a promise at graduation to stay connected. If nothing else, they all agreed to meet each year over the Memorial Day weekend for a few days on a bicycle tour. He put down his briefcase, changed into his exercise clothes, and headed for the gym. He remembered how much he enjoyed the first three bike tours they all took together. It was great catching up on life, work, successes, and problems.

The last time they met they talked about getting their careers started. Sam was just finishing up his final year of law school and was concerned about how he was going to start paying back his student loans. He had interned at good law firms all three years, but didn't have a job offer yet. Elliot had not found a job he really loved. He said it was hard to break into marketing so he was still working as a salesman for a local TV station selling advertising time. Joseph had just started a job in a small finance department for a local chain of privately owned supermarkets. Brian thought it would be good to see his friends; he did have some vacation time coming. He called each one of them back and started to make plans to join them on the annual bike tour.

They met at the hotel Sunday night at the beginning of the Memorial Day weekend. They checked in and got caught up over dinner. The four friends laughed over stories from college, talked about politics, and compared notes on their fourth year in the workforce. They'd had grand ideals when they graduated. They were going to change the world. Elliot and Joseph said they were doing fine. They had the same jobs as last year and their companies were doing well. They felt secure, which was a definite plus in this strained economy, but they wanted more. They didn't want to just get by; they wanted to make a difference. Sam never did get the job offer he was hoping for, but said it turned out to be the best thing that could have happened. He started working as a Legal Aid lawyer. Not only was he helping people every day, but his student loan debt was being extinguished through his state's loan payment assistance program.

Brian went last and told the group about his promotion. He talked about the changes at SBC and how they had rolled out very successful software recently. He was reluctant to talk more about his leadership lessons from his grandfather, and wondered how they would react to his GPS story. It was getting late and they had an eighty-mile ride tomorrow.

Monday's ride was beautiful: ten thousand feet high, surrounded by mountains, lungs filled with nothing but fresh air. It was hard work pedaling up that trail, but the views were worth the effort. They returned to their hotel in time for an early dinner and an evening of exchanging more stories about their lives.

It was reassuring how none of the four friends had changed since their days in college. Even their phone messages about the bike trip rang of their passion in life: Joseph, the finance major, loved the facts: when we are going, where we are going. Elliot, the marketing major, loved the experience: mountain climbs, views, and friendship. Sam, the lawyer, loved the agreements: our commitment to stay connected. Brian, the computer science major, loved the technology: all the different ways they could share information. That night's discussion was no different.

Joseph talked about his job at the local supermarket chain, H&H Schmidt. It was a family-owned business that started in 1915 when the founder, Henry Schmidt, emigrated from Germany to the United States. He started one store with what little money he had and ran it with his wife, Helen, and eventually his children. Now his grandchildren ran the company and had expanded to three stores. Joseph found ways to help them cut costs, earn more, and invest more in growing the business. "But this is the way we have always run the business," Joseph quoted the grandchildren.

Elliot got up out of his chair and patted Joseph on the shoulder as he walked to the window saying, "I have the same problem. Why won't they listen to our ideas?" After staring out the window for a minute, Elliot turned suddenly and said in an excited voice, his hands moving in the air, "Four guys ride by on their bikes in a close single file and you can hear the sound of their tires as they pass; whoosh, whoosh, whoosh, whoosh. Break to the setting sun over the mountains and you see the silhouettes of these four riders pedaling up to the peak. Fade out on the four men sitting on a porch smiling and laughing and the announcer says, 'Reconnect with nature and your friends on the California mountain bicycle trails.' Creating advertising, not selling advertising time; that's where I need to make my mark on the world."

Sam agreed with Elliot, "You do have a way of drawing everyone into a scene."

"Like the Raphael tapestries in the Sistine Chapel," Brian added.

"I know; I've tried pitching my big ideas to the television station managers. They remind me that my job is to sell the advertising time, not create advertising.

"What about you Sam? You seem to have found your dream job," Joseph said.

"You're right." Sam answered. "I am helping people resolve disputes they're having with landlords, banks, phone companies, hospitals, you name it. Sometimes I get involved with small-business owners who are having trouble collecting from their customers or paying their vendors. I get to do all of that and see my student loan balances decrease quickly. I should be satisfied. But I'm not. You see, I help folks out of one problem; I don't help them prepare for the next problem. It isn't unusual for me to see the same people again with the same problem or a new problem. I could really make a lasting difference if I helped them learn how to make better choices in the future."

Brian couldn't help but feel that he had heard this conversation before. It reminded him of that Monday seven months before, when Grandfather had told him to wait for the lesson on step four, about detours, before he tried to implement his vision and quick wins. He knew all he was learning about successful leadership would help him. Could it help his friends too, even though they were all in different businesses? He was not sure he should tell them what he had learned. There are ten steps over three phases and Brian had only just finished the first four steps in the first phase. He was definitely not an expert on leadership. He was also unsure how his friends would react if he told them his grandfather was talking to him through his GPS. He decided to just talk about his job and what he had accomplished without talking about the ten steps and how he had learned what to do.

Brian was proud to tell his friends about the three new products that SBC rolled out in the last seven months after his promotion. He said being the manager of a larger group of software developers was similar to being the lead programmer, but he now had the responsibility of his team's and the company's successes. He talked about working with the sales manager, and how he reassigned programmers to different parts of the projects. Brian described the new testing program he instituted and how it identified errors so they could be fixed before delivery. He ended by saying that the next product that SBC develops will be even better than the last three.

When he stopped talking, he noticed that his friends and several other cyclists in the room were on the edge of their seats, just staring at him. He realized that he had just given a presentation on SBC product development, as if he were in front of his team. He sat down waiting for his friends to say something.

"Who are you and what did you do with our friend Brian?" Elliot joked.

"It was like listening to Mark Zuckerberg talk about Facebook, or Howard Shultz talk about Starbucks. You sound like you're the CEO," Joseph added.

Sam joined in. "How is it that a computer programmer with only as much experience as the rest of us can be so confident talking about leading a group and making such a difference in a company? Where did you learn how to do that?"

Brian responded, "You remember me talking about my grandfather and all the stories about historical leaders he told?"

"Yes," they all replied.

"Well, it comes from those stories."

"Brian, you have to tell us those stories," his friends said together. "We want to make a difference the way you have."

"There is nothing I would like more than to help each of you. But I don't think I am ready to teach anyone how to be a successful leader. I have only been at this for seven months."

An older man cleared his throat rather loudly and said, "Excuse me. My name is John; I am on the bike tour with you. I couldn't help overhearing your conversation. Do you mind if I tell you a story that I think may help?

"Along with bike riding, I am a frequent hiker. All hikers know that you can't out run a bear. But these two guys were hiking in the deep woods one day. They got a bit off track and wandered into the part of the woods were bears have been known to live. ROAR! The frightening sound of a bear was heard. ROAR!! The sound grew closer. One of the guys bent down and started tightening his shoes. 'What are you doing?' the other one asked. 'Lacing up my shoes so I don't trip when I run,' the first one answered. 'Everyone knows you can't out run a bear,' the second one said. To that the first guy replied, 'I don't have to out run the bear, I just have to out run you,' and he sped away.

"Why did I tell you that story?" He looked at Brian and continued, "Young man, your friends asked you to teach them what you know about leadership, and you are hesitant because you don't know everything about leadership. In the story about the bear, you are the first guy who tightens up his shoes, your friends are the second guy, and knowledge about everything having to do with leadership is the bear. You don't have to know everything about leadership to teach your friends something about leadership. You just have to know more than they do."

Brian thought about what John said. He looked at his friends and said, "Okay, I will teach you what I know about leadership. We have four more days on our bike tour. We finish our bike climbs each day by 4:00 p.m. That leaves enough time for dinner and a lesson on leadership each night."

DEMONSTRATING LEADERSHIP LESSONS

Brian was glad he had synced up his leadership notes on the iCloud so he could view them on his iPhone. He would print his summaries at the hotel business center for his three friends to follow. As he was reading over his notes that night, he remembered what Grandfather said about using a language that is understood by the student to teach the paths to successful leadership. The driving lessons were Brian's language, but his friends might not so easily understand that analogy. He closed his eyes and thought about what Grandfather would do to teach his friends on this trip. Of course—the bike climbs would be the perfect parables for the leadership lessons. He would find a way to incorporate the day's climb into the four steps of leadership they would be learning.

The second day was another tough climb with great rewards: views of two beautiful lakes that one of the riders said were like the Swiss Alps. An easy, fast ride down brought the group back to the hotel with energy to spare for the rest of the evening. Brian and his friends had dinner and then found a quiet corner to begin their lessons in successful leadership.

He started with step one. Where are you going? He read the phrase that he and Grandfather would say together when he started his driving lessons. "You have to know where you're going. If you don't know where you're going, you will never know if you've arrived."

Brian and his friends talked about the purpose of the bike rides—to get to the top and then back down. He told Grandfather's stories about Dwight Eisenhower, Vince Lombardi, and Daniel Boone. He shared his own story about discovering the purpose for SBC.

Day three was one of the toughest climbs they had ever experienced. There were inclines as much at 13 percent at some points and a lot of uphill climbs. The ride down was no easier. A mixture of curves, humps, and some flat pavement made this a descent where they needed to pay attention. They were all glad that their guide had explained the terrain for them in the morning. When they reached the hotel they rested before dinner.

After dinner they met at their spot to study step two in successful leadership. Brian started, "Today's ride was the perfect example of step two. What are the conditions? Can you imagine taking today's climb and descent without knowing what you were in for?" The friends talked about some of the turns and hills that they never would have been able to handle if they hadn't known were just ahead. "Leadership is no different. You have to be prepared for what's ahead. The information you gather by looking, listening, and learning will be that on which you base all future steps to successful leadership."

Brian explained the processes that George Washington Carver and Michael Abrashoff used to determine the conditions in and around their teams. He finished with describing how he researched the conditions in and around SBC.

Day four consisted of a two-tiered climb back to back. First a twenty-two-mile climb up to ten thousand feet, followed by a steep climb up another four thousand feet. The second climb varied from miles of open road on the mountains with no protection from the heat to steep 15 percent climbs. On the descent they were pedaling against thermal winds that rose up the mountain and slowed them down. That day's climb succeeded in being even harder than day three. When they returned to the hotel they were tired, but not as tired as they would have been if their guide hadn't told them that the key to today's ride was many small climbs with quick rests in between.

After dinner, Brian led the discussion on step three in successful leadership. How are you going to get to your destination? "Just like today's climb, which we achieved as a series of small climbs, successfully achieving your team's purpose comes through a vision that consistently delivers small successes for each team member." Brian shared how he had wanted to change SBC as soon as he saw what needed to be changed but that he learned he needed to take a measured approach.

He talked about Robert F. Kennedy and how he changed history one act of courage at a time. Then he discussed Czech Republic President Vaclav Havel and said, "For your vision to be effective you have to set it in motion. This is called quick wins." Brian finished the lesson by showing his friends the vision and quick wins he developed for SBC.

The final climb, on day five, was nowhere near as steep as the first four days, but it did have twenty hairpin turns and other changes in the road direction that came upon you almost without notice. After this day's climb, their minds and eyes were more tired than their legs. Constantly looking ahead for the next change so it didn't take you by surprise was difficult, but as with all the rides, the scenery was beautiful.

The friends met for dinner for the last time. They took their places in the corner after dinner for their fourth lesson on successful leadership. Brian told them this lesson was titled "Be prepared for detours." He compared today's climb with its twists and turns to unexpected diversions that occur in leadership. "We were successful in today's climb because we knew the curves were coming. Since we had never biked on these mountains before, we didn't know exactly where they were going to be, but we knew they were coming. This lesson carries over to leadership. To succeed in reaching your destination, expect detours and have a plan to work around or through them."

Brian showed his friends the list of four detours on the road to success and the plan to work around or through them. He finished by sharing the details of his four detours.

With the bike tour and the leadership lessons over, Brian knew it would be some time before he saw his friends again. He felt he owed it to them to explain that this was not the end of the lessons on successful leadership, that there were six more lessons to be learned; only he didn't know what they were yet or when the next one would come. Brian decided to tell them about his grandfather and the GPS and whatever happened would happen.

"Before we head upstairs to pack and get our last night's sleep in this hotel, I have something to tell you. I have enjoyed being able to pass on these four leadership lessons to you. I told you they came from my grandfather's stories, and that is true. What I didn't tell you is that my grandfather is teaching me these lessons right now through my GPS.

"You see, he recorded ten lessons on successful leadership on my GPS before he passed away. He knew I would need them someday and he was right. My grandfather was a very wise man, and he programmed the GPS to know when I'm ready for each lesson. I have completed the first four lessons, which I shared with you. There are six more lessons that I will be learning over time. The four lessons you learned this week are enough for you to make a difference in your career; they were for me. But knowing my grandfather as I do, I can assure you that the best is yet to come. I would like to keep passing on the lessons on successful leadership as I learn them, if you are interested."

Brian's friends were a bit amazed. It was hard to understand how Brian's grandfather could teach him through his GPS, but what they did understand was that Brian had the success that they desired in their lives. They all agreed to meet the next time Brian contacted them. It might be over the phone, it might be in person, but they would connect and take this journey together.

RECONNECTING WITH GRANDFATHER

Brian arrived back at his apartment on Saturday evening. He unpacked and went to the grocery store. After church the next day he'd settle down at his desk, turn on the GPS, and try again to see if Grandfather would resume his lessons on successful leadership. For now, he was glad to be back in his own bed.

He talked to his pastor after the service on Sunday. The pastor wanted to know how Brian's bike tour went. Along with describing the scenery and how good it was to connect with his friends, Brian talked about teaching the leadership lessons that his grandfather had taught him. His pastor asked him to consider talking to the church leaders; they could benefit from those lessons. A week ago he would have politely declined that offer. But after last week's experience—and the bear story—he agreed to stop in one day after work.

He asked his pastor what he thought about a leadership course for the high school students in the church. His pastor liked the idea and said they would discuss it when he came in during the week.

It was an unusually warm June day and he was glad to get back to his air-conditioned apartment. He hoped that now would be the time to begin learning step five. He sat down and turned on his laptop and the GPS. He typed SUCCESSFUL LEADERSHIP into the GPS and as he was reaching to press GO he stopped.

"What if there is no response again?" Brian thought, "It's Sunday night, tomorrow I go back to work. I've followed all four steps and they worked. I don't know what to do next." He reached out and pressed GO.

"Welcome back, Brian," came Grandfather's voice. "You are now ready for the final step in phase one of successful leadership development."

"Yes I am!" Brian shouted out loud.

"In step five you will learn that the success of a journey often depends more on who you are with than where you are going. Step five teaches you to make room for other people to share in the success of your journey.

"I knew that you would take the first four lessons to heart. I am sure that your team is seeing the positive impact you are having on their lives, and the work you are leading is the best in your industry. But as odd as this sounds, that is not enough.

"You see, I am teaching you these lessons in leadership so you can be a river, not a reservoir. A river takes its water downstream, freely allowing it to flow to anyone who needs water. All who come in contact with the river are nourished by what it contains. A reservoir, on the other hand, is meant to capture and store water so it can be used someday for a specific purpose. As you invested your time in the success of your team, others noticed that success. By now you have begun to open up your reservoir of leadership lessons and nourish those who have sought out what you possess. Now you are ready to continue with your lessons."

Brian realized now why he had not heard from Grandfather sooner. The positive results he was going to see were not just for his team. After last week's bike tour his friends now understood the first four steps to successful leadership and could use them to really make a difference with the people in their lives. His pastor and the other church leaders would be able to use the steps to help them make a difference. Maybe the leadership class for the high school students would take off and make a difference in their lives too.

STEP FIVE: MAKE ROOM FOR OTHERS

Grandfather continued, "Let's review where we were in your driving lessons. I said that the first five steps are the preparation for driving. You know your destination; you understand the conditions of your car and the roads; you have decided on a route and have the suitcases, snacks, and music in the car; you are ready for the detours that may come. The final step of preparation for the family vacation trip was to make sure that everyone is in the car.

"It sounds simple, but the day you leave for a family vacation car trip is hectic. People are in and out of the car and in and out of the house. There are the last minute bathroom stops, and the final questions: Is the gas turned off on the stove? Did you stop the mail and the newspaper?

Do I hear water running in one of the sinks? With all that confusion it would be easy to drive off and leave someone behind in the house. That's why we always took a roll call to make sure everyone was present and in their proper seat before driving away.

"You are in the same place on your leadership journey. You have completed the first four steps of preparation. You know your team's purpose; you understand the conditions of your team, your industry, and the economy; you have decided on a vision and have selected quick wins to implement your vision; and you are ready for the responses to change that will come. The final step of preparation for your leadership journey is to make sure your leadership team is in place.

"By following the first four steps to successful leadership, you have already made an impact on the lives of your team, and others have noticed. You have set the wheels of success in motion and the demands for you and your time will be coming faster. Up to this point, you have directed each quick win. Nothing happened without your personal involvement; that is the way the first four steps are designed. You brought your team where they are today, but you can't bring them any further on your own. If you want to extend the positive results beyond what your team is accomplishing now, you will need to make room for others to share in the success of your leadership journey.

"Ronald Reagan, the fortieth president of the United States, said one of the keys to successful leadership is to 'Surround yourself with the best people you can find, delegate authority, and don't interfere as long as the policy you've decided upon is being carried out.'

"Leaders who desire to be successful will discover that they need other leaders to carry out their vision. Some will discover this in hindsight, when they don't follow this advice and the success of their vision is limited. Others will discover this through the extensive success that occurs when this is done right. So how do you do this right? Delegation of authority is serious business. It requires that you trust the other leaders with the authority to implement your vision. Before you hand over that authority you must decide on the qualities of a person whom you would trust to implement your vision, and then you look for the people with those qualities.

"Bill Walsh was the head coach of the San Francisco 49ers during their 1980s dynasty. When he took over as the head coach in 1979, the 49ers had a losing record in five of the last six seasons with the most recent season at two wins and fourteen losses. Walsh described the qualities of leaders to whom he would delegate his authority to implement his vision. 'During this early period I began hiring personnel with four characteristics I value highly: talent, character, functional intelligence (beyond basic intelligence—the ability to think on one's feet, quickly and spontaneously), and an eagerness to adopt my way of doing things, my philosophy.'

"Successful leaders may call these qualities by different names, but each one has the same four qualities for their leadership team: common principles, environmental experience, practical successful background, and diverse strengths."

Brian didn't doubt that Grandfather was right about this. He welcomed the idea of being able to delegate authority. He had been so busy leading everything himself that he was losing the connection with his friends. He was eager to learn the right way to keep making a difference at SBC and with the other opportunities that were opening up.

COMMON PRINCIPLES

"What do I mean by common principles?" Grandfather asked. "When you delegate your authority to other leaders on your team, you want to feel secure that that leader intends to use the authority in a way which you would approve. Thomas Jefferson said, 'In matters of style, swim with the current; in matters of principle, stand like a rock.' Having common principles does not mean that you surround yourself with other leaders who could be mistaken for your mirror images; we will discuss why this is not a good idea later under diverse strengths. But there are certain expectations of leaders from which you cannot waiver.

One principle that we would all agree on is honesty. Mary Kay Ash, the founder of Mary Kay Cosmetics, started with one store and a five thousand dollar investment. Today, Mary Kay Cosmetics generates over two billion in sales and has been named one of the one hundred best companies to work for in America. Mary Kay said, 'Honesty is the cornerstone of all success, without which confidence and ability to perform shall cease to exist.' Here are some of the other principles that must be viewed positively by your leadership team: integrity, character, ethics, teamwork, motivation, and respect. There can be more, but these will lay the foundation for your success. The fact that I am teaching you the importance of these common principles should tell you that you will not find these in every person. Be diligent as you decide to whom you delegate authority to implement your vision."

Brian thought about the principles Grandfather listed as he wrote them in his notes. He had heard of Mary Kay; he remembered his mother and sister talking about their makeup and pointing out the pink Cadillacs on the road. He didn't realize the story behind the company, but thought it was tremendous that his lessons crossed so many different industries. He summarized his notes, writing: *Common principles are needed everywhere, but are not common in everyone.*

ENVIRONMENTAL EXPERIENCE

"Now on to environmental experience, a fancy way of saying that phrase I used to hear from you and your friends: 'Been there, done that.'

"You have to trust that your leadership team will use good judgment on every decision they make. Fred Brooks, the man who managed the development of IBM's System/360 family of computers knows a thing or two about good judgment, he wrote the book on it. Brooks wrote about his experiences managing systems development at IBM in the book *The Mythical Man-Month: Essays on Software Engineering.*

"The IBM/System 360 was the first fully compatible family of computers designed to cover a range of applications from small to large. This allowed customers to choose the right model for their use and upgrade to larger systems as their needs increased without the time and expense of installing new software. The book coined what is known as 'Brook's law,' which states that 'adding manpower to a late software project makes it later.' Brooks discovered this law when he himself added more programmers to a project falling behind schedule, then concluded that it delayed the project even further. Using this and other examples of what he learned in his career, Brooks is quoted as saying,

'Good judgment comes from experience and experience comes from bad judgment.'

"Any leader to whom you want to delegate authority should have experience in the environments they will be facing. The internal environment of a large public company is different from that of a small private company. The internal environment of a thriving organization is different from one that has stalled or, worse yet, is on the decline. The internal environment of a start-up is different than an established company. Similarly the external environment is different when the economy is growing than when it is shrinking, and the external environment is different for a highly regulated industry than for a private industry. Experience doesn't guarantee success, but it does offer opportunities to learn from past mistakes."

Brian turned off the GPS, got up from his desk, and walked over to his bedroom closet. After rummaging through some boxes he hadn't looked in since he moved to his apartment, he found *The Mythical Man-Month* by Fred Brooks. Brian's professor in his systems development course used this book to demonstrate the counterintuitive nature of systems development. He had written a note inside the book for each student to remember; "Sometimes, your first reaction to problems can be the best solution, but sometimes it can be the worst. This book contains some of the classic mistakes that developers have made in the past and unfortunately continue to make now. Learn not to make the mistakes that others have made; there will be plenty of time to make mistakes of your own."

Brian remembered how much he enjoyed that course. His professor was a lot like his grandfather. He had a knack for making his point in a phrase, or a story, like the story of Fred Brooks. Now it had all come full circle; the same story was being used for a different purpose. Brian had avoided some of the system development mistakes that Brooks discussed in his book as he developed software. Now it wasn't the specific mistakes that were the focus, it was a larger message. Brian wrote: *Those who have learned from past mistakes—their own or others'—are better prepared to lead than those who have never experienced mistakes at all.*

PRACTICAL SUCCESSFUL BACKGROUND

Brian turned on the GPS again to continue his lessons.

"'Been there, done that' was a familiar phrase I borrowed from you to describe environmental experience," Grandfather said. "A practical successful background adds to the environmental experience that is needed, so let me describe this requirement for a leader to successfully carry out your vision by completing that familiar phrase 'Been there, done that' and adding, 'got the T-shirt.'

The leaders to whom you will delegate your authority must have a history of success in the responsibilities of the role they will be filling on your team. Former Green Bay Packers coach Vince Lombardi said, 'Winning is a habit. Unfortunately, so is losing.' How does winning become a habit? Sarah Knowles Bolton, a press correspondent and author of the late 1800s, wrote several books that summarized the lives of successful people: statesmen, artists, and scientists, to name a few. In her research she found that 'the victory of success is half done when one gains the habit of work.'

When you find a leader who has a history of success, that leader also has a history of dedicated work to achieve that success. This does not mean that you can only delegate to leaders who have held the exact same job in the exact same industry as you. But it does mean that their successes should demonstrate a mastery of the strategic skills that will be required for their particular role."

Brian recognized this in his own promotion. He didn't have the title of manager in his background, but he did have a history of hard work and success in leading software development projects. He summarized his notes and wrote: *Leaders with a history of success have developed a habit of working hard to achieve their success.*

DIVERSE STRENGTHS

"The final requirement you will look for in a leader before you delegate your authority is diverse strengths," Grandfather said. "The famous psychologist Abraham Maslow said, 'If the only tool you have is a hammer, you are likely to perceive every problem as a nail.' What he meant by that oft-used phrase is that an individual is limited by their knowledge and experience in their ability to offer solutions to problems. Each person has a diverse set of strengths formed by their abilities, knowledge, and experience. When these diverse strengths are used together, the ability to offer multiple solutions to problems becomes possible. An ancient Japanese proverb sums this up well: 'All of us are smarter than one of us.'"

As Brian summarized his notes, he couldn't think of a better way to describe the need for diverse strengths than the Japanese proverb; he wrote: *All of us are smarter than one of us.*

Brian turned off the GPS and summarized the four qualities for a leadership team. He took a break for dinner, knowing that there was more to come on this lesson; Grandfather had not given him his next assignment yet.

ASSIGNMENT

Brian sat down after a quick dinner, typed SUCCESSFUL LEADERSHIP into the GPS, and pressed GO.

"Now that you understand the need for delegation and have an idea of the general requirements of a leadership team, it's time to take a step back and look at the organizational structure of your team," continued Grandfather.

"Start by assuming that you are designing your structure from scratch. Assume that there is no structure today—no leadership team and no employees. The key to your next assignment is to design the structure and fit your team to the structure, as opposed to building a structure to fit your team. Don't worry; your team isn't going away. You will find that most of your team will be in the same roles but with a better understanding of their part in the success of the team. The few who do change roles will thrive as their new roles better match their strengths.

Keep a clear focus on your purpose and vision for achieving your purpose and analyze which unique functions belong together in separate groups within your organizational structure. Think of these as teams within your team or companies within a company. Each one has a role in your vision for achieving your purpose. They all have a unique product to deliver, which must fit together with the other unique products in order to deliver one product to your customer. I call these centers of excellence. Once you have your centers of excellence in mind, apply the four qualities for a leadership team.

Common principles are common across your whole team; this should be the same regardless of the center of excellence. Each member of your leadership team will be operating in the same environment, so their environmental experience should closely match your current environment. Successful practical experience and diverse strengths will be unique to the center of excellence you have designed. When your ideas for the centers of excellence are clear and you have a firm grasp on the four qualities for your leadership team, estimate how many team members will be needed in each center of excellence. When you complete this assignment, I will give you your final assignment that will complete the five steps in phase one of successful leadership. One last word of advice on this assignment: take enough time to complete this well, but not too much time. You will find that the success you experienced through the first four steps will guide you to the answer."

Brian turned off the GPS and felt his energy level renewed again. He had the next assignment he was longing for and could hardly wait to complete it. He wanted to stay up late and finish it tonight, but doubted if that would meet Grandfather's definition of enough time.

He spent the next week thinking about this lesson, his first four steps, the success they had achieved, and observing his team in action. The seven common principles that Grandfather mentioned were already apparent to him in his interactions with Dan and many other team members. It was easy to work with Dan and the others who embraced these principles. Brian understood the environment his leadership team would encounter at SBC from his work in step two on conditions and from how the responses to change came in step four. The vision and quick wins from step three seemed to be the most important factors in the success his team had achieved. His leadership team would need a practical, successful background and diverse strengths to continue the success they developed following his vision and quick wins.

Of course; that was what Grandfather meant when he said, "the success you experienced through the first four steps will guide you to the answer." Brian already had the centers of excellence designed; they were in his vision and quick wins. His four centers of excellence were the customer needs and solution center, the prioritization and project management center, the software development center, and the delivery control center.

It was easy to estimate the team members needed for each center of excellence. Brian saw this at work over the last seven months as he implemented his quick wins. There were a few more team members needed at this point. As they specialized in each of the quick wins, the process improved. Most of the extra work that needed to be done was absorbed into the more efficient process. But some of the team members were dividing their time between two roles. Brian finished the week confident that he had completed his most recent assignment well.

FINAL ASSIGNMENT IN PHASE ONE

Saturday morning after his usual run by the lake, Brian hurried to the GPS. He was eager to receive his final assignment and complete the five steps of phase one. He typed SUCCESSFUL LEADERSHIP and pressed GO.

"Brian, you've made it," came Grandfather's warm welcome. "You are now ready for the final ascent to the top of phase one of successful leadership. I am confident that you will be just as successful in this last assignment as you have been in all of the others. Remain diligent, don't cut corners. This will complete phase one.

"Remember what I said when we started your leadership lessons. Phase one is the foundation for all you will do and accomplish. Without success in phase one you will not be able to move forward through the next two phases. You and your team will be frustrated that you're unable to accomplish more than you can personally direct. Your final assignment has two parts.

"First, you will present your plan for the centers of excellence to your boss to obtain his approval. This is important because you will need the budget dollars to carry out your plan, but it is also important to demonstrate that you are still part of the larger team whose interest remains with helping the team succeed. Your boss may ask questions and challenge your new structure; that is to be expected. I did that with my leaders when I ran businesses to make sure they had thought the entire structure through. Answer the questions honestly and confidently. You will find that the success that you achieved in your quick wins will have smoothed the path for approval for your plan.

"The second part of your final assignment is to hire your leadership team. This sounds easier than it sometimes can be. Here is how it should be done. There are four sources you can use to locate candidates for your leadership team. In order of preference, they are: your current team members, people you know from past experience, referrals from current team members, and external recruiting. Using the four qualities for a leadership team as your guide, you should evaluate candidates from the four sources, in the order I prescribed, until your leadership team is complete. Invest the appropriate amount of time interviewing each person to ensure you select the best candidate for the role regardless of whether they are on your team already or if you are meeting them for the first time.

Similar to your first assignment on step five, I advise you to take enough time to complete this well, but not too much time. This advice is important because you will be measuring each candidate against the standard you defined using the four qualities for a leadership team.

"Based on my experience, I think it is unlikely that you will find one candidate who possesses all of the qualities as described. My rule for dealing with this situation was to 'Look for the Dids and the Coulds and decide which Dids you need and which Coulds you can build.'

"I know you are asking what that rule means. Here is how I decided who the best candidates were for my leadership roles. For each new role, I ranked the four qualities into must haves and nice to haves.

"I can tell you that in my must-haves column were always common principles and a practical successful background. I believe that qualities such as honesty and hard work are qualities that someone brings with them as opposed to being taught on the job.

"I would evaluate the need for diverse strengths based on the particular leadership role being filled. If the role was in an area in which I had little if any strength, then I would rank diverse strengths in the must-have column, given my lack of expertise in that area. Otherwise it was a nice to have.

Finally, I almost always ranked environmental experience in the nice to have column if my other must haves were present. I figured that I could invest my time in teaching a leader how to operate in our environment if I didn't need to spend my time in the other areas. Brian, you are now ready to proceed to your final assignment."

"Brian summarized his notes for this lesson and wrote: *Good leaders look at people's strength and make use of it; Great leaders look at people's potential and make the best of it.*

FOUR QUALITIES FOR A LEADERSHIP TEAM

COMMON PRINCIPLES
Common principles are needed everywhere, but are not common in everyone: honesty, integrity, character, ethics, teamwork, motivation, and respect.

ENVIRONMENTAL EXPERIENCE
Those who have learned from past mistakes—their own or others'—are better prepared to lead than those who have never experienced mistakes at all.

PRACTICAL SUCCESSFUL BACKGROUND
Leaders with a history of success have developed a habit of working hard to achieve their success.

DIVERSE STRENGTHS
All of us are smarter than one of us.

FOUR SOURCES FOR RECRUITING A LEADERSHIP TEAM

- Current team members
- People you know from past experience
- Internal referrals
- External recruiting

GAINING APPROVAL OF THE PLAN

Brian scheduled time with Arthur to review his plan. He came prepared to tell his story and to demonstrate why this was the logical next step. Keeping in mind Arthur's motto of doing the job you have been given to do, he reviewed his team's goals for the year and how he had met each one ahead of schedule with more successful customer and employee feedback. He described his four centers of excellence and how, with his plan, he would help SBC obtain more revenue and profit and help the employees enjoy more professional success.

Arthur asked a few questions about how the teams would work together and not see themselves as separate. Brian answered by talking about how each leader's goals would be tied to the total success of each product, not just their piece. He also described his team-building plans including meetings, lunches, and community outreach events. Arthur had to admit that he had seen positive changes at SBC. Brian's plans were approved.

BUILDING THE TEAM

Over the next month he interviewed all of the internal candidates from SBC. He was a bit surprised that a few of the applicants were from outside of his team; he didn't realize how word of his team's success had spread. He received some applications from the small-business sales department and some from outside of the small-business division. Using Grandfather's rule, Brian was able to fill three of his four leadership roles.

Madeline, the leader of the customer needs and solution center came from the small-business sales group. She was part of the initial team during the quick wins and was a great team player full of energy. Along with sales experience, she had been a successful programmer at SBC earlier in her career. She had management experience but lacked the experience in building a new team. Brian was confident that he could invest his time mentoring her on that quality.

He didn't find a leader for the prioritization and project management center. Several candidates had some of the four qualities of a leadership team, but they all lacked the practical successful background. During their quick wins, he had to run this area himself. If this center of excellence was going to succeed, it needed someone experienced in project management. This was not an area in which he was competent to teach to a leader. He would need to continue looking for candidates from the three other sources.

He filled the remaining two leadership positions from inside his team for the software development center and the delivery control center. Li was a former peer as a lead programmer for another product. He was well respected as a programmer by those he led in development. He was a good fit to lead software development even if he didn't have strengths that were diverse from Brian's.

Eduardo came from the programming team. He had developed the new testing program they had used on the last three products. Prior to SBC he had several jobs building software testing programs at larger firms. He hadn't led the testing groups, but had good ideas about leadership. The delivery control center was going to be the smallest of the teams and Brian felt he could invest his time teaching him management and leadership.

For the last position, he followed Grandfather's advice and thought about people he knew from past experience. His only experience outside of college was at SBC and he had interviewed everyone he thought might be qualified at SBC. His college friends were not in the software field so he moved onto the third source for leaders, internal referrals.

He asked his team members if they knew anyone they would refer for the open leadership role for the prioritization and project management center. He received several referrals and followed up on each one of them over the next two months.

Eduardo recommended a former colleague named Hugh. He said, "I have a really good sense of what you're looking for, since you hired me. Hugh would be perfect for this role. He had the same job at my prior employer." Brian arranged to talk to him and found out during the interview that he still liked his job, but Eduardo had spoken so highly of SBC that he wanted to hear more. He did have all the qualities that were needed for this role. Hugh accepted the offer to join the team because he was excited to be part of building something new again. He said, "My current job has grown stale; they've lost that passion for achievement and are satisfied with their large market share."

With that final position filled, Brian's leadership team was in place. He had reached the top of the mountain of phase one.

PHASE ONE—RELATIONSHIP
The Relationship Built Through Leadership Is Remembered Long After Understanding and Knowledge Are Imparted.

Step One: Where are you going?
You have to know where you're going. If you don't know where you're going, you will never know if you've arrived.

Step Two: What are the conditions?
The information you gather by looking, listening, and learning, will be that on which you base all future steps to successful leadership.

Step Three: How are you going to get to your destination?
Successfully achieving your team's purpose comes through a vision that consistently delivers small successes for each team member.

Step Four: Be prepared for detours
To succeed in reaching your destination, expect detours and have a plan to work around or through them.

Step Five: Make room for others
The success of a journey often depends more on who you are with than where you are going.

PHASE TWO—UNDERSTANDING

The understanding of what success looks like comes from modeling yourself after those who have successfully achieved the outcome you desire.

CHAPTER EIGHT

SHOW THEM HOW IT'S DONE

THERE'S NO BETTER TEACHER THAN OBSERVING SUCCESS IN ACTION.

Brian woke up early Saturday morning to get a head start on his leadership lessons with Grandfather. His leadership team was in place, which completed his final assignment in phase one of successful leadership development, and this was going to be a busy weekend. He wanted to learn as much as he could today. Tomorrow he'd drive to his parent's house after church to kick off a special Labor Day weekend.

It had been two years since he'd seen his sister, Karen, her husband, Alex, and his nephew, Jackson. Alex's job had taken them across the country but they would be in town all week to visit both sides of the family and some friends. Jackson was only five and a half when they moved. Brian remembers the 'and a half' Jackson would say when Karen said how old he was; now he was about to turn eight. He was looking forward to seeing Karen and Alex, but he really missed watching Jackson grow up. Karen was good about sending pictures and letters, but there's just no substitute for being together. There would be enough time for reminiscing over the next two days. Now it's time to get back to his leadership lessons.

He looked at the notes he'd taken when Grandfather began his leadership lessons. He thought about Grandfather's golfing story. In phase one he established trust by building relationships. He told his team where they were going and they saw the results in the quick wins. He realized that the trust and relationships didn't end with his team. He had also built relationships and established trust with Dan, the sales force, and Arthur. Brian turned on the GPS, typed SUCCESSFUL LEADERSHIP and pressed GO.

STEP SIX: SHOW THEM HOW IT'S DONE

"Congratulations, Brian," Grandfather's reassuring voice said. "You have completed phase one of successful leadership development. You have set the foundation well for you and your team's future growth. When we started, I told you that phase one was the preparation for phases two and three. After achieving success in all of the five steps of phase one, it is difficult to believe those were just preparation for success. Remember, I have been where you are. I told you earlier that with success in phase one you will be tempted to stop moving forward and miss reaping the benefits of changing lives in a big way. There were lives changed in phase one, but that was just the beginning and it can be so much more.

"Abraham Lincoln, the sixteenth president of the United States, said, 'Give me six hours to chop down a tree and I will spend the first four sharpening the axe.' If you spend four hours sharpening the blade of an axe, you will have a very sharp axe; that in and of itself is a successful endeavor. You took a dull axe and successfully turned it into a sharp axe. But if the ultimate goal was to clear a forest so you could find the best land, build a home to protect your family, and plant crops that could feed generations, the successfully sharpened axe was just the beginning.

"Let's return to your driving lessons and step six, the first of the three steps in phase two, will become very clear.

"After we reviewed the preparation for our family car trips, I felt that you had learned well. You could plan your own trip when it was time. The trip we took in the summer I was teaching you to drive didn't involve the whole family. Your grandmother and I had just purchased a conversion van and we invited you and your sister to join us on a drive to the beach for the month. Karen was about to start her senior year in college and we wanted to really connect with her before she graduated and headed off into her adult life. It was also a chance for your parents to spend time together, just the two of them.

"You and I were up front together. Karen and your grandmother were in the back looking at vacation pamphlets and talking about life—girl talk. Your job was to be the navigator and I was the driver. I didn't need to teach you how to use the GPS; you already knew how to use it better than anyone. If we wanted to make a stop to eat at a certain restaurant, or visit a local attraction, you could find it in no time. I used all of the information you provided as I drove; but recognized that I was still in control of the wheel. You were playing an important part as the navigator, but we would not arrive at our destination if I was not steering the car.

"The goal of your driving lessons was to delegate driving the car to you. If I always kept control of the wheel, you would never learn how to drive. I needed to show you how I drove. I needed to tell you what I was thinking as I drove; what I was paying attention to as I drove. I needed to show you how to drive by my example. Albert Einstein said, 'Example isn't another way to teach, it is the only way to teach.' This is why phase two is called Understanding—the understanding of what success looks like comes from modeling yourself after those who have successfully achieved the outcome you desire.

"As I drove us all to the beach, I explained what I was doing and why I was doing it. I talked about how I checked the traffic before entering the highway; how I accelerated into the lanes; how I kept aware of the cars and trucks around us; and how I made sure I could see the car on the right in my mirror before I pulled back into the right-hand lane. It became a game for you and me as we tried to be the first one who spotted something on the road that a driver should be aware of. When we decided to exit the highway for a stop I would ask you what I should be doing to prepare. We continued this activity into town as I asked you to direct me to our hotel on the beach.

ASSIGNMENT

"You are now at step six of successful leadership: Show them how it's done. Each of your leaders is responsible for one center of excellence just as you were responsible for navigation on our trip. You hired them for what they already know and for where they can go with your leadership. You can delegate responsibilities that are their strengths right now, and show them how to do the rest.

"Your assignment for this step is to keep leading your teams to success as you did in phase one. Use the same quick wins, or new ones if needed, to demonstrate your vision. Continue to have meetings, plan projects, and deliver your purpose. But now, invest time with your leadership team explaining how you lead in each situation and the benefit of your approach. This is how you begin the process of delegating leadership."

Brian turned off the GPS and checked the clock—just enough time to summarize his notes on this lesson before heading out to meet some friends downtown. He wrote: *There is no better teacher than observing success in action.*

THE PICNIC

Sunday after church, Brian stopped at the grocery store to pick up potato chips for the picnic on the way to his parents' house. He arrived just in time to welcome Karen, Alex, and Jackson and help them get settled in his and Karen's old rooms. He dropped his bag in the basement. Other than a night on the couch, this was just like when he was a kid. They stayed up late making s'mores at the fire pit in the backyard, and Brian talked about what had been happening in his life.

They left early on Monday to get their favorite spot by the lake for their Labor Day picnic. It would be a day of jet skiing, hot dogs, Frisbee, and baseball. Jackson is the pitcher on his Little League team and Brian couldn't wait to throw the ball with his nephew. At lunch they continued catching up.

Alex is a pilot and he likes being based in a city with an airport hub. He is home more often since he doesn't have the connecting flights on each trip. It gives him time to be involved with Jackson's Little League. He isn't much of a ball player, but he is good at math, so he keeps the statistics on the teams.

Karen is a teacher's aide in Jackson's school and leads a women's Bible study at church. She is home with Jackson every afternoon and enjoys helping the teachers during the week. The impact of the Bible study took her by surprise. The lives of the bible-study ladies were changing before her eyes.

Jackson took some grapes out of the bowl, stood up and said, "Watch me, Uncle Brian," as he tossed them in the air one at a time and caught them all in his mouth one by one.

"I showed him how to do that," Alex said proudly.

Karen rolled her eyes and no one was sure if they should clap or gasp. She stood up, mussed Alex's and Jackson's hair, and started to laugh. "My boys!" The whole table broke out in laughter.

Jackson grabbed his baseball mitt and ball. Who's up for catch?" he said as he tossed another mitt to Brian.

"I guess that would be me," Brian answered.

They both ran out to the baseball diamond and started throwing the ball back and forth. "You've got quite the arm," Brian said to Jackson after another stinging heater. "I've been practicing. I throw the fastest ball in the league,'" Jackson replied as he threw the fastest ball yet.

"Uncle Brian, can I ask you a question?"

"Sure, anything."

"Well, some of the other guys in my little league are starting to pitch curveballs. Mom said you were a pretty good pitcher when you played baseball. I was wondering. Would you teach me to pitch a curveball?"

Brian stopped just as he was about to throw the ball back. "Your mom said I was a good pitcher? I didn't know she was paying attention."

"Well, technically, she said you were a pretty good pitcher. But what do you think? Will you teach me?"

"Okay, no big ego here, it's not like I'm a professional player, but I still remember how to throw a curveball. I'd be happy to teach you."

"Before you start, you should know that my dad already taught me all about wind resistance and how the ball has to spin for it to curve. My dad is really smart and the best pilot in the sky. But knowing how it's supposed to work didn't help it work. I still can't throw a curveball."

"Your dad took care of the complicated stuff," Brian said as he walked Jackson to the catcher's box, "We get the easy jobs. I show you how to hold and release the ball and you imitate me using that strong arm of yours."

Brian demonstrated how to grip the ball with the middle and index fingers together on top of the widest part of the seams. "See how the ball doesn't touch the palm of my hand? I rest the ball on my ring finger and thumb. You grip the ball with your middle finger and thumb on the seams and your index finger rests on top of the ball as a guide." He turned his hand around so every side of the ball is visible. Jackson tried to grip his ball the same way and Brian moved his fingers around until he had it just right.

"I don't have to teach you the next step, my hand is still sore from catching your fastballs," Brian said, rubbing his glove hand. "You wind up and throw the ball with the same natural motion and speed as a fastball. But the angle of the ball as it comes out of your hand is what makes the difference. The palm of your hand should face inside, like a karate chop, until you release the ball. Then you should follow through just like a fast-ball, across your body. Don't make the common mistake of snapping your wrist to give the ball spin; all that does is injure the pitcher's arm."

Brian threw a few curveballs to Jackson, then let him try. With the right technique, Jackson was throwing curveballs in no time. They both returned to the picnic and Jackson ran to tell his dad that he could throw a curveball now.

As he thought about what had just happened, Grandfather's lesson made perfect sense: if he wants to delegate the implementation of his vision to his leadership team he has to show them how it's done.

DELEGATION

Brian returned to work on Tuesday ready to begin the process of delegation. His team was already working on the next products by going through the process established with his quick wins.

Until now Brian had been running the product development projects. Now he could delegate the day-to-day management of the activities of each center of excellence to his fully capable leadership team.

He announced a new meeting schedule. Their quarterly meeting for the whole team to share the stories of success would remain the same but they were adding two new weekly meetings.

The first was for him and his four leaders to keep them all focused on their long-term strategy and their short-term goals. Each leader would provide updates on their piece of each project to the team. They would talk about their vision, the industry, and review customer and employee survey results.

The second was for individual time with each member of his leadership team. These would be more personal and geared to the specific development needs of each leader. Here they'd review the week's activities related to each center of excellence. They'd discuss what went well and what could be improved. They would also prepare for the next week's activities and discuss what they wanted to accomplish. Over the next several months, he and his leadership team became better connected. They gained a greater understanding of Brian's vision, and gained a greater understanding of their strengths and needs.

Madeline, the leader of the customer needs and solution center, caught on well. Her knowledge of sales and development and her desire to learn allowed her to grow as a leader in her role. Brian taught her about trust, relationship, and the first four steps of successful leadership development. The quick wins for her team started to take hold and bring success.

Hugh, the leader of the prioritization and project management center, was everything that Eduardo said. His team was progressing very well under his leadership. His project management skills were far better than Brian's, which was just what was needed. Brian invested time with Hugh to ensure that the vision was clear and then let him lead his group.

Li, the leader of the software development center, reminded Brian of himself when he was first promoted: a great lead programmer who wanted to be a great leader. Brian worked with Li just as Grandfather worked with him: one step at a time with assignments to practice and develop leadership skills.

Finally, the testing under Eduardo in the delivery control center was on schedule, continuing to ensure that the products were error free. Brian offered more direction to Eduardo as he taught him the foundations of management.

As Brian was leaving work on Friday, he received a text message from Joseph, his friend from college. He said he would be in town attending a seminar next week and wondered if they could meet for dinner one night.

Brian called him when he reached his apartment. Joseph said the four leadership lessons they learned on their Memorial Day week bike tour worked well; too well, in fact. Six months ago no one would listen to his ideas. Now after following the four steps he had been so successful that everyone was coming to him for ideas. He was promoted to the manager of the finance group and couldn't keep up with all the demands. "Brian, I need to know what your grandfather would say about my situation," he pleaded. They decided to meet Monday night for a quick dinner at the hotel where Joseph was staying. "Get ready to take some serious notes," Brian said. "You'll find the answer you are searching for."

PHASE TWO—UNDERSTANDING

The understanding of what success looks like comes from modeling yourself after those who have successfully achieved the outcome you desire.

Step Six: Show them how it's done.

There is no better teacher than observing success in action.

CHAPTER NINE

TAKE YOUR HANDS OFF THE WHEEL

THE FIRST STEP IN LETTING THEM GROW IS TO START LETTING THEM GO.

Monday after work Brian drove to the hotel and sat down in the lobby. They were supposed to meet at six and it was about to pass six thirty. He went to the front desk and asked them to call Joseph's room. No one answered. "This is strange," he thought, "He's never late. I'll wait for another fifteen minutes."

"Yes, the order was placed; I just did it myself...no problem...glad I could help..." Joseph ended his cell phone call as he walked into the lobby and sat down next to Brian. "There are days when I don't think anything would be done if I didn't do it all myself. Sorry I kept you waiting. This is it; this is my life right now. The grocery stores are doing so well that I have trouble being out of the office for a day, even to attend a seminar that will help me do my job better."

Brian stood up, reached out, and took his hand. "Let me help you up." In the restaurant they sat down at a quiet corner booth so they could talk while they ate. "I want to hear all about the success of your four steps," Brian said and reached into his briefcase for a pen and notebook.

"I thought you would ask that," Joseph said. He opened his binder, took out two sets of papers, and passed one across the table. "I remembered how prepared you were on our bike tour when you taught us the first four steps of successful leadership. You gave us a full set of pre-printed notes that summarized the four steps right there in the Sierra Mountains.

"I started just as you said we should. I looked for information that already existed about the economy and the industry; I listened to the owners and employees whom I interviewed and to the customers through an informal customer survey in the store; and I learned what was needed by analyzing the two together.

"I discovered that the purpose for the H&H Schmidt Grocery Store is to deliver food and other goods that people need and want while generating sufficient profit. The external conditions are difficult; unemployment is high, the cost to produce and ship the food is rising due to recent droughts and high gas prices. Competition is divided between the mega-stores like Wal-Mart, specialty stores like Whole Foods, and local grocery stores like ours. The mega-stores have lower costs because of their buying power and the specialty stores have unique goods that can be sold for a premium.

"The employee morale at Schmidt was pretty low. Turnover was high because the employees want a path to more responsibility and money, and everyone knew that the only store and department managers were members of the Schmidt family. Each store manager ordered their own store's goods from suppliers to keep local control. To offset the rising costs, they reduced their inventory, kept prices higher, and stopped refilling open employee positions. Because of this, shelves were starting to run empty.

"I found that customers loved the local-store feel and the history at Schmidt. But they were leaving because they needed the goods they needed at a good price and the store ran out too much. They also missed the employees who kept leaving, and their children needed part-time jobs, but the pay was better at other stores.

"Brian, I borrowed your phrase about SBC when I designed my vision for Schmidt's Grocery: imitation is preferred when you are following success and innovation is preferred when you are defining success. I believed we could be more successful if we were a local store with mass appeal for what is needed and local appeal for what is wanted. I thought we should price high volume 'needs' competitively for a reasonable profit and price lower volume 'wants' higher for a greater profit. We should hire and train local people with knowledge of local needs and wants and a connection to the community."

Joseph stopped talking when he noticed the waiter standing at the table. "Is your food all right?" he asked. Neither of them had eaten a bite, they were too busy with their lesson. They nodded and began to eat.

When the waiter was a safe distance away, Joseph returned to his story. "I then moved onto the quick wins that I could control. Since I prepared all of the reports for finance, I built a new tracking and forecast report that analyzed sales of goods across stores. It showed the different costs and prices for the same basic goods at each store and which items were selling out each month. I added a section that showed the additional profit that would result from obtaining the lowest current cost from the suppliers and highest current price to the customers at a quantity that kept the shelves full. I took that report to my boss, who was impressed and asked me to present this at the store managers' next monthly meeting.

"All of the store managers were surprised; they had never looked at their results this way. I suggested that this all could happen if we centralized ordering and pricing to be competitive with the larger mega-stores that use their buying power with suppliers for the basic goods. I showed the managers how the profit would still be much greater than today if they hired more employees at a higher rate and maintained more loyal employees and customers. They all agreed that centralized ordering was a good idea for the basic goods, but they still liked the local feel and wanted to keep control of their specialty goods themselves. I then showed them the part of the new report that focused on specialty goods. I highlighted the local goods that were not selling as quickly in each store and the cost savings of lowering the order quantity of these items while maintaining the same sales volume.

"Right there on the spot they promoted me to the new position of manager of finance and strategy. They asked me to be responsible for all of the centralized ordering along with my finance job. They also asked me to expand the analysis and reporting of the stores' sales and profits and report back each month on any new strategic opportunities. I started to talk about the employee morale and promotions when my boss, who also heads human resources, said he would talk to me about the employee suggestions later.

"Over the last six months we centralized ordering, and pricing and profits have doubled. I present my analysis each month and we make decisions each month that will keep profits increasing. We have also turned the local specialty sections in each store into a real attraction. It brings in customers just to see what local farmers and companies are producing. Customers are happy to pay a higher price to support their community. We raised the pay of our employees and turnover has slowed. I did face some of the detours you told us about, but I was prepared to keep my focus on the vision. I haven't had time to work with my boss on ideas for training and development, but maybe after I implement the next step you are going to teach me I can introduce him to your grandfather's lessons."

BEING A RIVER

Brian put his pen down and clapped. "Congratulations on the success of the Schmidt Grocery Stores," he said. "I'm thrilled that my grandfather's lessons helped you just as they helped me. I want to reassure you that I was just where you are when I completed the fourth step. The first four steps were designed so that nothing happened without your personal involvement. This was meant to establish trust in you and your vision. I gather from our phone call on Friday and your cell phone call in the lobby that you and your vision are trusted to bring success to your team and your company."

"You're right," Joseph replied, "I am busy because the four steps worked. You said there were ten steps. I think I need the next step to rise above having to do everything myself."

Brian took out his notes on step five. "Now it is time for you to take notes, Joseph. When I reached the time for step five, Grandfather said he knew that I had had an impact on the lives around me and that success was noticed. He said demands for my time had increased and would be increasing rapidly from now on. I remember one statement he made that really summed up the choice I had to make—the choice you need to make, Joseph. He said, 'You brought your team to where they are today, but you can't bring them any further on your own. If you want to extend the positive results beyond what your team is accomplishing now, you will need to make room for others to share in the success of your leadership journey.' For you to continue your journey requires that you trust other leaders with the authority to implement your vision. Not just any other leaders, but a select team of leaders with the right qualities that you will hire and personally teach.

"There are four qualities necessary for a leadership team to be successful: common principles, environmental experience, practical successful background, and diverse strengths. Each of these qualities is important to analyze as you design your organizational structure into centers of excellence…"

Over the next two hours, Brian helped Joseph design his organizational structure. They discussed the team that Brian hired and their qualities. Joseph talked in more detail about the different responsibilities he had and divided them into centers of excellence. Brian finished the lesson with his advice on how to present this new idea for approval and how to locate candidates through each of the four sources.

As they left the restaurant Joseph said, "I don't know what I would do without you and your grandfather's lessons. I can't thank you enough for investing your time with me. What can I do to repay you?" Brian stopped and turned to look at Joseph. "My grandfather said that he was teaching these lessons to me so I could be a river and not a reservoir. He expects me to share this with anyone who asks. I am asking you to do the same."

"I can do that. Just like the man on the bike trails said, I don't have to know everything, just more than someone else in order to teach them. Sam is getting along well and I will share this lesson with him. But Brian, you have to call Elliott. He called me a couple of weeks ago and was very disappointed in his job. We all heard the same lessons and they worked for me, but not for Elliott. I told him I was going to call you to learn the next step and he could join me. He didn't want to hurt your feelings by telling you the four steps didn't work for him and one more step wouldn't help." Brian patted Joseph on the back and walked to his car.

Brian called Elliot after work on Tuesday. "Joseph and I met last night."

"I know, Joseph called me from his hotel room and said you would call," replied Elliot. "He said you two had a great lesson and he knew exactly what to do next. It's okay, I was just not meant to be a leader."

Brian remembered that phrase; I was not meant to be a…He used that when he was young and failed at something. Grandfather would challenge him to keep trying to do something he had never done before.

"Before we come to that conclusion, let's go over what happened. Tell me about the purpose of the television station and the conditions you are operating in. Tell me about your vision and quick wins." After a long pause, Elliot replied, "I can't do that."

"Why not?" Brian asked sympathetically.

"Look, I made a mess of things at work. I didn't follow all of the steps just like you said. I took shortcuts. I already know about our competition; I have to sell against them every day, and I have personal experience in how difficult the economy is right now. My ideas would make a difference, if the station heads would just implement them.

"When I returned to work after our bike tour I approached my boss and pitched my ideas again. Once again he said that I should keep selling advertising, not creating advertising. It's too late now; I had my chance to use your four steps."

"You did take some shortcuts," replied Brian. "When I was in a situation similar to yours, my grandfather told me the story of a man who thought it was too late.

"This man was so busy building his house that he didn't have any time to plant trees. When he finished the house, he became occupied with his job and couldn't take time away to plant trees. He met a woman at work; they married and had a daughter. His life became so busy with his family that he didn't have time to plant any trees.

"One summer day he was outside playing in his backyard with his daughter; the bright sun was making them both very hot. 'Daddy,' she said, looking up with her hand on her forehead to shade her eyes. 'Why don't we have any trees in our yard?'

"He thought about what his daughter asked and replied, 'I guess I was always too busy to plant any trees. I'm sorry I didn't plant any when I built the house. It's too late now. Even the fastest-growing trees would take at least five years to reach a height that would give us shade.' To which his daughter replied, 'Daddy, in five years I will only be eleven years old. I'll still want to play in the backyard with you then, and I'll still want shade from the trees then. So you're right, the best time to plant trees would have been when you built the house. But the second best time to plant those trees is right now.'

"Elliot, now is the second best time for you to follow the steps to successful leadership." They talked late into the night. They went over the four steps again and discussed the success that Joseph obtained following them in order. They determined the purpose of the local television station, evaluated the conditions of the industry, and brainstormed ideas for a vision and quick wins. Elliot left with his assignment to implement the first four steps and committed to following Brian's advice.

STEP SEVEN: TAKE YOUR HANDS OFF THE WHEEL

Over the next few days Brian thought about his time with Joseph and Elliot as he continued to show his leaders how it's done. He was glad he could help them get back on track but wondered how he would ever be able to fully delegate his vision. If his leadership team was like his friends, it seemed that they would continue to need his help.

Saturday morning Brian took his spot at his desk in his apartment, turned on the GPS, typed SUCCESSFUL LEADERSHIP and pressed GO. Out came Grandfather's familiar voice. "The seventh step of successful leadership is one of the most exciting—and at the same time one of the hardest—steps you will take as a leader.

"You will begin to let go of the control that you have over your team, just as when your child rides their bike for the first time without training wheels. You run next to them, holding onto the back of the bike until they get up enough speed, then you do it…you let go of the bike and they ride as you run right behind them.

"This is just what I did in your driving lessons when you and your sister joined your grandmother and me at the beach for the month. The next step is called "Take your hands off the wheel." Step seven required that I move to the passenger seat and let you get a feel for driving on your own. In step six, I gave you an example of how to drive. In step seven you will begin the process of trying to drive on your own.

"Sophocles, the fifth century Greek playwright, said, 'One must learn by doing the thing. For though you think you know it, you have no certainty until you try.'

"At this step you were not ready to drive off on your own. There was still practice to be had and teaching to be done. If I had let you go at that point without my continued direction, you might have made mistakes that could cause a serious accident. You sat in the driver's seat and I watched as you started the car, backed out of the driveway, and drove down the road and around the town.

"I occasionally reminded you of what you had learned in the first six steps, and I often complimented you on your driving skills. I was there like the autopilot of a plane to move you back on course if you veered away.

ASSIGNMENT

"Brian, you are now ready for your next assignment with your team. Take your hands off the wheel, move to the side and let them get the feel of leadership. Just as in step six, you will keep doing what you have been doing: have meetings, plan projects, and deliver your purpose. But now, let your leaders take the lead. Let them run the meetings and projects and make decisions. Stay close by their side to remind them of all that they've learned and compliment their leadership skills. You will be letting go soon enough."

Brian's experience with Joseph and Elliot made sense now. Just as with his leadership team, he was their autopilot. They weren't ready to lead on their own, but they would be in time.

He summarized his lesson on step seven and wrote: *The first step in letting them grow is to start letting them go.*

When Brian returned to work on Monday he began letting go of the wheel. For the next several months he listened to his leaders and helped guide their decisions. He reminded them of what they had learned as they prepared for significant meetings, then he stepped back and allowed each of them to lead their meetings as he made coaching notes for later discussions. Each of his leaders was continuing to grow in their roles.

Madeline excelled in the customer needs and solution center. Her team trusted her and looked to her as their leader. He made some suggestions as they planned their strategy for the upcoming product, but mostly he watched and complimented her leadership in meetings, with sales, and with her team.

The prioritization and project management center was just about running itself these days. Hugh had become the go to person for project management in the company. Brian continued to remind Hugh to stay focused on the vision, but remain flexible if priorities change. The project meetings were running smoothly and Brian asked fewer questions than before, complimenting Hugh on how prepared his team was on each project.

The software that Li and his team in the Software Development Center turned out got better with each product; they were surely the best in the industry. Brian continued to work with Li to become more of a leader and less of a lead programmer.

Eduardo and the delivery control center were undefeated; no product rolled out with bugs since he took over. His management skills were developing well and Brian was starting to work on more strategic leadership lessons.

Brian was very pleased with the progress his leadership team was making. He saw the day coming soon when he would be able to fully delegate implementing his vision.

PHASE TWO—UNDERSTANDING

The understanding of what success looks like comes from modeling yourself after those who have successfully achieved the outcome you desire.

Step Six: Show them how it's done.

There is no better teacher than observing success in action.

Step Seven: Take your hands off the wheel.

The first step in letting them grow is to start letting them go.

CHAPTER TEN

LET THEM DRIVE

CONFIDENCE IN ONE'S ABILITIES INCREASES WITH EACH SUCCESS.

The weekends were more relaxing now that the day-to-day operations were under control. It was time to check with Grandfather and see if his leaders were ready to lead on their own. Was Brian ready to learn step eight? He typed SUCCESSFUL LEADERSHIP into the GPS and pressed GO.

"Hello, Brian. As I record this, I am looking at the picture of you and me on the day you passed your driver's license test. Do you remember that day?"

"Of course I do," he replied. "I've looked at that picture here on my desk while I learned every step."

"That day will be part of your lesson today, but only the beginning," Grandfather said."

STEP EIGHT: LET THEM DRIVE

"The first seven steps of your driving lesson prepared you for that day. You were ready to take your driver's license test and receive the document that said you were ready to drive on your own. As you drove me home, we discussed how receiving the license let you legally drive the car by yourself; but as of that moment, you had never really been fully responsible for the operation of any car. I told you that to be a great driver you needed to build your confidence in driving alone, and that I would help you.

"As much as we liked to talk together, I knew you were disappointed to hear that your driving lessons weren't over. I told you the story of Jerry West. He was a small boy who was kept away from children's sports to keep him from getting seriously hurt. Shooting baskets in his neighbor's backyard was his escape. Throughout his life, he practiced so he could be the best. As he reached high school, he grew healthier and became an all-state player. He went on to college and was an all-American player.

"West played fourteen years for the NBA Los Angeles Lakers and was called 'Mr. Clutch' for his ability to make big plays in clutch situations. During his professional career he was voted twelve times to the all-NBA first and second teams and was elected to the NBA all-star team fourteen times. After he retired he was inducted into the Basketball Hall of Fame and voted as one of the fifty greatest players in NBA history.

"When speaking of his success in basketball West said, 'Confidence is a lot of this game or any game. If you don't think you can, you won't.'

"Jerry West gained his confidence from doing what he wanted to be confident in doing. Likewise we worked to build your confidence in driving alone, by having you drive alone on short planned trips.

"You were excited to practice driving alone, and I had many errands that I could have you complete: grocery store, gas, post office, to name a few. Before each short journey, we talked about the first seven steps and how you would use them to safely drive there and back. After each short journey, you returned with a report on your trip. Your short journeys turned into longer journeys until your confidence soared. You moved from 'I think I can' to 'I know I can.'"

Brian remembered those practice trips well. He quickly learned that planning before the trip to remind him of what he had learned and reviewing the trip with his grandfather helped him become a more confident driver.

ASSIGNMENT

"Your leadership team is in the same place as you were. They have learned the first seven steps in successful leadership and it is time for them to begin to lead on their own. Step eight is called 'Let them drive.'

Your assignment is to help them develop the confidence they will need to be great leaders by letting them lead one journey at a time.

"The same meetings will happen, projects will be planned and the purpose of the team will be delivered. But this time you will give the responsibility for these leadership journeys to your leaders. Your part is now to help them plan for the short journeys they will take on their own, and review their experience after they return. As their confidence grows, their short leadership journeys will become long leadership journeys and soon they will be leading on their own.

"Eleanor Roosevelt said, 'A good leader inspires people to have confidence in the leader; a great leader inspires people to have confidence in themselves.'"

Brian summarized his notes for step eight and wrote: *Confidence in one's abilities increases with each success.*

THE TEACHER BECOMES THE STUDENT

Spring break had arrived. Joseph, Elliot, and Sam arranged a ski week in Colorado so the four friends could celebrate becoming great leaders. Brian was ready for a break and would begin step eight when he returned to work the next week.

Sam was a ski instructor in high school, and Joseph and Elliot had skied for years. Brian wasn't much for cold weather and had never been on the ski slopes. This year would be his first spring break vacation in the snow. His friends said it was only right that they teach him to ski after all he had taught them about leadership.

They checked into the ski resort around two in the afternoon with plenty of time to hit the slopes. The three experienced skiers packed their equipment and headed to their rooms to change. Brian stopped by the rental shop to pick up his equipment for the week. Being a new skier, he was a bit unsure on his skis, but he thought he would do just fine; he was athletic and kept in good shape. They all met at the lodge at four.

"Off we go to the bunny slopes," shouted Sam rounding up the four friends.

When they arrived Sam put on his best instructor look and used his best instructor voice.

"Before we start to ski there are a few steps we have to review for your safety. This will be especially important for anyone of you who have never skied. First, can anyone tell me the purpose of skiing?"

"I can," answered Elliot, "To make it down the hill with no broken bones."

"You or anyone else on the hill," added Joseph as all four of them laughed.

Sam got his composure and continued, "Okay, we will try to be serious. The next step is to examine the conditions of the slopes. Are they powdery or slick? Are you on a steep hill or one like this bunny slope? Then we check our equipment. Are your boots snug and attached to your skis correctly? Are the straps on your poles in good shape so you won't lose them?

"All right, for you beginners, it's time to learn how you are going to get down the slopes: the snowplow. This is how you will make it to the bottom of the hill without crashing into people along the way or at the bottom.

"The first step is to make a forward facing V position with the tips of the skis being closer together than the tails. To slow your speed, bend your knees and put more pressure towards the tips, and to increase speed, rest back. To turn, put more pressure on the opposite ski of the direction you want to turn. To turn left, put pressure on the right ski; to turn right, put pressure on the left ski. More advanced skiers can use the parallel turn and the hockey stop. For beginners, we will practice this throughout the week and you will find that you won't need the snowplow by Thursday.

"And of course, there will be skiers skiing or falling directly in front of you all day; keep your eyes out for them, and maintain a controlled speed so you can stop or go around them.

"We will practice on the bunny slope tonight, and tomorrow we will all head over to the green circle slopes so you beginners can get used to a steeper grade. Don't worry; I will be right beside you until you are comfortable with the speed. By the end of the week we will all be riding the lifts to the blue squares and you will be skiing on your own.

"Everyone to the rope tow," Sam announced to his class, and they all started up to the top of the bunny hill. "Follow me and I will demonstrate the snowplow down this hill."

Brian followed the instructions and was having a great time. He only fell once, which gave him the opportunity to learn how to get back up;

something that was harder than it seemed. He appreciated his friends skiing with him and encouraging him on the bunny slope. They were all good enough to ski the black diamond runs but said helping him succeed was thrill enough for this trip.

At dinner they exchanged stories of their careers. It had been almost a year since they were all together on their Memorial Day weekend bike tour. They had grown so much personally and felt like they had really made a difference in the lives of their teams and coworkers. Even more amazing was that during these difficult economic times, their companies' sales and profits were growing.

Elliot took the floor with his usual flair for the dramatic and said, "Only four months ago I couldn't have joined this conversation. I thought I could do it my way. I resisted following the advice of those who had successfully achieved what I desired. Since I stepped out onto the path to success, my footing is secure and my vision is clear. Brian, I think I can speak for the others when I say, lead on. We are ready for your grandfather's final five lessons on successful leadership."

With that he took a bow like a Shakespearean actor as the others clapped and shouted, "Bravo, bravo."

"Do you remember how I used our bike tour as a means of teaching the first four lessons?" Brian asked.

"Yes," they said, nodding.

"Well, our ski trip is another perfect example of how the ten steps to successful leadership work. As Sam was teaching us—"

"Excuse me—us?" Joseph interrupted.

"Okay, let me try that again. As Sam was teaching me how to ski, I couldn't help but see the similarity between his lessons on skiing and our lessons on leadership, which makes sense if you think of our illustrious ski instructor as the leader of the team.

"Step one was the purpose: to make it down the hill without breaking any bones. Step two was the conditions: powdery or slick snow and equipment. Step three was the vision of how to reach the purpose: snowplow for beginners, parallel turn for advanced. Step four was the detours: skiers falling in your way. And step five was who was going to be skiing with me: my three good friends.

"I have still not learned all ten steps, but I have learned steps six, seven, and eight. However, I would be honored, dear sirs, to share the wisdom contained in those three steps." Brian finished, imitating Elliot's Shakespearean delivery.

"We are now beginning phase two of successful leadership," he continued. "In the first five steps of phase one, you became a great leader. In phase two, you are modeling the way for your leadership team to become great leaders.

"Sam already taught you step six earlier today on the ski slopes when he said, 'Follow me and I will demonstrate the snowplow down this hill.' In this step, you will show your leaders how you lead, just as Sam showed us how he skis. Keep doing what made you and the team successful, but now you explain each step to your leaders so they understand how it's done.

"In step seven, your goal is for your leaders to experience how true leadership feels. We haven't experienced this step yet on our ski trip, but it is coming tomorrow. 'We will all head over to the green circle slopes so you beginners can get used to a steeper grade. Don't worry; I will be right beside you until you are comfortable with the speed' is what I heard tonight.

"Just as in step six, you will keep doing what you have been doing, but let your leaders take the lead. Stay close, remind them of all that they've learned, and compliment their successes."

"I didn't know I was this good," Sam boasted.

"How about we say you are good at using the steps to leadership and continue with the final step for the night—step eight," replied Elliot.

"Great segue, thanks," Brian continued. "Step eight will be the final lesson for the night and the final thing we do on our ski trip. As I said, I have not learned steps nine and ten. As a matter of fact, I haven't implemented step eight yet myself, but based on the success of the first seven, I am sure it will work.

"Sam said, 'By the end of the week we will all be riding the lifts to the blue squares and you will be skiing on your own.' And that, my friends, is step eight. Your leaders need to lead on their own.

"Your goal in step eight is to help your leaders build confidence in their ability to lead. Their confidence will increase with each success. And just as in steps six and seven, you will keep doing what you have been doing, but now you will give the responsibility for these leadership journeys to your leaders. Your part is to help them plan for their short journeys and review their experiences after they return."

The rest of the week was better than expected. They all mastered the blue squares and the friends parted promising to return with the black diamonds as their goal.

Brian returned to work invigorated and excited to implement step eight. He had already seen this step in action for himself on the ski slopes. Over the next six months he worked with each of his leaders to help them build their confidence in their ability to lead.

He no longer attended the product strategy meetings. Madeline discussed issues with him before the meetings and they reviewed the decisions made during the meetings, but this was her meeting and her responsibility.

Once the team agreed on product prioritization, Hugh led the project management. If issues arose, Brian trusted that the solution would be brought to him for approval.

Li was responsible for assigning developers, and managing his team's workflow. He brought new ideas for solving programming needs to the staff meetings for questions and suggestions before implementing.

If bugs were found in testing, Eduardo and the delivery control center worked with Li to correct them. Brian monitored the issues and got involved if there were going to be show stoppers, but his leaders ran the process.

Step eight was just as successful as all the other steps and phase two was complete. Grandfather was right when he said that lives would be changed in phase one, but there was so much more. Brian had seen his leadership team develop into great leaders who were fully dedicated to the success of their center of excellence.

PHASE TWO—UNDERSTANDING

The understanding of what success looks like comes from modeling yourself after those who have successfully achieved the outcome you desire.

Step Six: Show them how it's done.

There is no better teacher than observing success in action.

Step Seven: Take your hands off the wheel.

The first step in letting them grow is to start letting them go.

Step Eight: Let them drive.

Confidence in one's abilities increases with each success.

PHASE THREE—KNOWLEDGE
The knowledge of when to apply what is understood comes through the side-by-side journey of mentorship

CHAPTER ELEVEN

IS EVERYONE BUCKLED UP?

THE SUCCESS OF A TEAM
DEPENDS ON THE SUCCESS OF
EACH MEMBER OF THE TEAM.

Brian's leaders developed confidence in their abilities over those last six months as they completed step eight. He was now able to invest his time almost completely in building his leadership team; they were really running the day-to-day operations of their centers of excellence without him. He felt that it was time for his next lesson, time to move on to the final phase of successful leadership development.

Once again seated at his favorite place, his desk in his apartment on Saturday morning, he typed SUCCESSFUL LEADERSHIP into the GPS and pressed GO.

"Welcome back, Brian," said Grandfather's voice, as clear and excited as the day they started. "You are almost finished with the ten steps to successful leadership development. I am proud of you for diligently following each step along the way. That is why you have achieved the success that you enjoy today, and your team has benefited from your success.

STEP NINE: IS EVERYONE BUCKELED UP?

"Earlier in our lessons I told you that step seven, take your hands off the wheel, was going to be one of the hardest steps because you were beginning to let go. You are about to take step nine where you are starting final preparations to let go completely. You need to know that this is the hardest step. Many leaders before you have stopped right here.

"I told you that Admiral James B. Stockdale said true leaders are '... men of the heart who are so helpful that they, in effect, do away with the need of their jobs.'

"Only the most confident of leaders can accept this challenge and believe the rest of the admiral's statement, which says, 'Leaders like that are never out of a job, never out of followers. Strange as it sounds, great leaders gain authority by giving it away.'

"Phase three is called 'Knowledge.' The knowledge of when to apply what is understood comes through the side-by-side journey of mentorship. In this phase you will be mentoring your leaders so they can be ready to lead on their own. You can, and probably will, continue to mentor some of them as they advance in their careers, but after phase three you no longer will be able to direct their actions, or be the autopilot to quickly move them back on course. They will set their own course and lead their own teams toward their vision.

"In phase one, you were responsible for everything that happened with your entire team. You were the one-and-only leader. It wasn't until near the end of this phase that you built your leadership team. In phase two, you continued to lead but showed your leaders how you did it. Gradually they took over the responsibility of their teams and developed confidence in their ability to succeed as you had. Now it is time for them to carry on the success you started by using their own strengths.

"John Buchan, the former governor general of Canada, author of over one hundred books, and former director of the Thomas Nelson & Sons publishing company said, 'The task of leadership is not to put greatness into people, but to elicit it, for the greatness is there.'

"You laid the basic foundation of leadership in phases one and two. In phase three, you will add to that foundation to guide them in beginning their own successful leadership journey.

"Let's talk about your driving lessons to help make this step clear. We ended with you earning your license and taking many practice journeys to build your confidence in your ability to drive alone. I was very comfortable that you could make good decisions, drive the car safely, and return from your chosen destinations.

"At some point in the future as you continued to drive, you would have passengers in the car with you. I told you that as the driver of the car you were responsible for everyone in the car arriving safely at your destination. That is why step nine asks: Is everyone buckled up?

"I told you that you were responsible for more than just the safe arrival of your passengers. Each passenger expected and deserved a ride that they enjoyed. This meant you had to pay attention to the air temperature in the back, the choice and sound level of the radio station, and smoothness of the road. Each passenger had expectations for the journey, no matter how short or long, and it was up to you to deliver.

ASSIGNMENT

"I know that you have done this for your team already. You have especially focused on your leadership team to ensure their success. That is what the last three steps were all about. Your assignment is to teach your leaders to do for their team members what you have done for them. They must take ownership for the satisfaction of the employees in their center of excellence.

"Change your mentoring sessions with your team to be discussions about their team morale and development. Encourage them to hold their own individual meetings with each of their team members. Review the results of the employee surveys with them and discuss opportunities for improvement.

"Jack Welch, the former CEO of GE knew something about growing leaders to lead on their own. Among a stellar list of former GE leaders who became successful CEOs in their own right are: Jim McNerney of Boeing, David Cote of Honeywell, Stanley Gault of Goodyear, Matt Espe of IKON, and Tom Tiller of Polaris Industries.

"In speaking about leadership, Welch said, 'Before you are a leader, success is all about growing yourself. When you become a leader, success is all about growing others.'"

Brian summarized this lesson and wrote: *The successful journey of a team provides success for each member of the team.*

On Monday morning, Brian received the Gallup employee-engagement score results. This was the first full year of results for the new team. He planned an afternoon meeting to discuss the results with his leaders. They had invested quite a bit of time in each other and with the entire team. This would be a great opportunity to really measure their progress as a leadership team.

The team had already heard him discuss how important these results would be. He quoted Grandfather, saying, "No matter how well your team is performing, and no matter how much your team likes you as a leader, they are hesitant to tell you what could be improved in one-on-one conversations."

The results were encouraging. On a scale of one to five, with five being the best, their overall score was 4.0. Brian's leadership team overall score was 4.75 showing that his personal involvement in their success had been recognized. He would use this information along with the individual results for each center of excellence to help his leaders build plans for continued improvement in employee satisfaction.

He began the new format for the individual meetings in which they discussed employee morale and development. He reviewed each team's Gallup results and development plans for the year with each of his leaders. Over the next four months he mentored his leadership team to begin getting them ready to lead without him.

Madeline's score in the customer needs and solution center was excellent at 4.50. Her experience and desire to learn had propelled her team to great group and personal results over the last year. She had already completed her second year of development goals with her team members and was growing future leaders. They discussed her team's organization structure and the need to think about opportunities for some of her team to take on more management responsibilities in order to groom them for the future.

The prioritization and project management center, under Hugh, also scored well at 4.0. In reviewing the detailed results, there appeared to be a small number of issues about technology and teamwork that were a concern for the team. They worked together on a plan for focus groups to understand the issues and build a solution to increase employee satisfaction.

Li and the software development center team's score was also excellent at 4.25. The verbatim comments indicated that some on his team thought he was a wonderful leader, but at times too involved in helping them complete their work. They felt their growth was limited because Li gave them the answers instead of helping them come up with the answers on their own. Brian continued to work with Li to become more of a leader and less of a lead programmer.

The score for the delivery control center was the lowest but still good at 3.85. Being a new manager, Eduardo expected the results to show room for improvement. He and Brian reviewed the reports in detail and developed a plan to continue growing his leadership abilities and team satisfaction.

PHASE THREE—KNOWLEDGE

The knowledge of when to apply what is understood comes through the side-by-side journey of mentorship

Step Nine: Is everyone buckled up?

The success of a team depends on the success of each member of the team.

CHAPTER TWELVE

DEFENSIVE DRIVING

IT'S NOT ABOUT RIGHTS; IT'S ABOUT RESPONSIBILITY.

Susan, the head of human resources at SBC, left a message for Brian on his office phone. She wanted to talk to him about mentoring and would schedule a meeting for later in the week. He wasn't sure what this was about. He was mentoring his leadership team and his college friends, but why would human resources want to talk to him about that?

On Wednesday, Susan came to his office to talk. "We're starting a new mentoring program for our managers. Your success has been noticed by senior management and you were recommended by Arthur. Would you be willing to start mentoring some of the other managers?"

He didn't know what to say. It was quite the recognition to be asked to mentor other managers. A recommendation from Arthur—who would have thought that would happen when this all started? What would Grandfather say he should do? He would say to be a river, not a reservoir, and pass on the knowledge. But this was different. In phase three he was supposed to be mentoring his leaders so they would be ready to lead on their own; this could divert his attention away from that goal. And not the least of his worries, he was the youngest of the managers with the fewest years of experience at SBC. How would they react to his suggestions?

"I appreciate the confidence you have in me," Brian responded. "Can I let you know on Monday? I want to look over my schedule to make sure I would be able to commit the time necessary for this mentoring to be a success."

"Of course," Susan said. "I'll come back then to hear your answer. I hope you can find time to fit this in. It would be a great help to these managers and to SBC."

Saturday seemed to take longer to come this week. It wasn't the mentoring of his leadership team that caused this; he enjoyed seeing them grow and rise to the challenge of becoming leaders on their own. The time passed more slowly because he had a decision to make and he knew the answer would come in step ten, his final lesson. He thought about his journey as he stared at the picture on the desk in his apartment. Whenever he came to a crossroads, the Leadership GPS had the answer. One last time, he typed SUCCESSFUL LEADERSHIP and pressed GO.

STEP TEN: DEFENSIVE DRIVING.

"Congratulations, Brian. You have just taken the first step on what promises to be an exciting journey to successful leadership development," Grandfather said, repeating what he said when they started the lessons.

"I know what you're thinking right now. This was supposed to be lesson ten, the end of the journey. Why did I just say you have taken the first step? Let's get right into step ten and you will see.

"The review of your driving lessons is almost complete. At this point you had earned your license and were driving on your own. You knew and followed the rules of the road; the car to the right goes first at a four way stop, pass on the left on the highway, turn right on red unless marked otherwise, and all the rest. I had complete faith that you were a good driver, safe and considerate. But to be a great driver, you need to do more than take care of yourself and your passengers. You need to watch out for everyone on the road. Step ten is called 'defensive driving.'

"Children may run into the street after balls, even though they shouldn't. Other drivers may pass through an intersection when the light has already changed to red. You may have to stop as a car backs out of the driveway right in front of you. Pedestrians may walk across the street when their light says to stop. Other people may not follow the rules and set the stage for their own harm.

"Driving defensively means that it isn't enough for you to follow the rules yourself; you need to be on the lookout for the best interest of others and do what you can to protect them from harm. Be an example to other drivers when you yield your right of way to another.

"A great leader of the American Revolution demonstrated step ten in his heroic leadership: General Gilbert Lafayette, better known as the Marquis de Lafayette of France. Without his actions, the United States of America might not be the free nation that it is today.

"He was born in 1757 and raised by his paternal grandmother after his father died. She taught him to take care of the poor, and he thought of himself as the protector of the peasants in the region. Even as a child he was rugged and drawn to the outdoors. He led the local school children on adventures through the woods and into ravines. He was left a wealthy orphan at age twelve, when his mother and maternal grandfather died and he inherited the family fortune. He continued to feel he was called on to perform great acts and became a soldier.

"Lafayette was trained in the French army and took his place in royal society as a frequent guest in the circle of Marie Antoinette. But in 1776, hearing of the American Revolution, he determined that his place was not in the luxury of nobility, but in the noble fight for freedom. In 1777, at the age of twenty-one, he used his wealth to buy a ship. Against Louis the Fourteenth's orders, he sailed to America. There he joined General George Washington as his aide-de-camp.

"Lafayette proved himself to be a capable soldier and leader who was well respected by his men. His upbringing in the fields and mountains of the French countryside made it comfortable to join the American pioneers who fought for their freedom. By 1781, the French government had announced its support for American freedom. Washington placed Lafayette in command of three regiments of infantry. He and his soldiers trapped the British, and when the French fleet arrived, a blockade was set up in Yorktown. Washington's forces joined the battle to defeat Cornwallis and end the Revolutionary War.

ASSIGNMENT

"Why did I say that with this step you had just taken the first step on what promises to be an exciting journey to successful leadership development? An ancient Chinese proverb says, 'By accident of fortune one may be a leader for a time, but by helping others succeed one will be a leader forever.'

"The success you have achieved will open many doors for you to share your knowledge and help many others succeed. Your assignment is to be an example of leadership that will inspire others to follow, just like Lafayette."

Brian stopped the GPS to summarize this last step and wrote: *It's not about rights, it's about responsibility.* He typed SUCCESSFUL LEADERSHIP and pressed GO for the last time to hear the end of Grandfather's lessons.

"With that we will end this journey together, but I will never be far. Remember I told you that I programmed the paths of successful leaders into your Leadership GPS and it can now anticipate and direct each turn you need to make. I look forward to joining you on your next journey."

Brian knew just what to do. He returned to work on Monday and agreed to mentor the other managers.

PHASE THREE—KNOWLEDGE
The knowledge of when to apply what is understood comes through the side-by-side journey of mentorship

Step Nine: Is everyone buckled up?
The success of a team depends on the success of each member of the team.

Step Ten: Defensive Driving
It's not about rights; it's about responsibility.

JUST THE BEGINNING

It's been three years since Brian took over the small-business accounting software group at SBC. His team has released many successful products and he has developed four great leaders. Most of his time is dedicated to mentoring his leadership team and several managers in other divisions. It's Friday at 4:00 p.m. and he is reviewing the week's accomplishments and setting next week's goals when a knock comes on his office door.

When the door opens, in walks Arthur, followed by SBC's president, Bill, who says, "Brian, we are here to congratulate you."

"Thank you, but for what?"

"Two things, really. First, for all of the success you brought to SBC over the last few years. You have done a remarkable job. Second, for your promotion."

"What promotion?"

"The promotion I am about to offer you right now. I have decided to start a new division focused on large-business clients; Arthur here is going to take that job and I would like you to lead the entire small business division. What do you say?"

Brian's thoughts raced. "Lead a whole division—this sounds like the offer of a lifetime. Grandfather said that doors would open for me to share my knowledge. Is this the right door?

"Madeline is ready to take my current job, so that isn't a problem. But I had experience in accounting software development before I took my first leadership role. I don't have any experience with the rest of the software groups.

"One of the first leadership lessons I learned was that most people are genuinely convinced that their situations are so unique and so difficult that no one has faced quite the same circumstances before, let alone found a way to solve them. But it doesn't need to be difficult. Eighty percent of most problems have been solved before; the other 20 percent is taking the initiative to accept the solution given to you and implementing it.

"I've been part of successful leadership in software development, financial strategy, advertising, and Legal Aid work. I saw the steps to leadership development demonstrated in my youth-service team, sailing, pitching, skiing, and of course my driving lessons. Most importantly, I have the Leadership GPS to guide me."

Brian stands up and shakes Bill's hand. "I accept."

Several weeks later Brian holds his first meeting with the heads of each small-business software group. He says, "Leadership is like driving a car. You have to know where you're going. If you don't know where you're going, you will never know if you've arrived…"

APPENDIX

THE THREE PHASES OF LEADERSHIP

Phase One	Phase Two	Phase Three
Relationship	Understanding	Knowledge
Think and See	Think and Do	Do without Thinking
Tell Me	Show Me	Involve Me

TEN STEPS

PHASE ONE—RELATIONSHIP

Step One: Where are you going?

You have to know where you're going. If you don't know where you're going, you will never know if you've arrived.

Step Two: What are the conditions?

The information you gather by looking, listening, and learning, will be that which you base all future steps to successful leadership.

Step Three: How are you going to get to your destination?

Successfully achieving your team's purpose comes through a vision that consistently delivers small successes for each team member.

Step Four: Be prepared for detours

To succeed in reaching your destination, expect detours and have a plan to work around or through them.

Step Five: Make room for others

The success of a journey often depends more on who you are with than where you are going.

PHASE TWO—UNDERSTANDING

Step Six: Show them how it's done.

There is no better teacher than observing success in action.

Step Seven: Take your hands off the wheel.

The first step in letting them grow is to start letting them go.

Step Eight: Let them drive.

Confidence in one's abilities increases with each success.

PHASE THREE—KNOWLEDGE

Step Nine: Is everyone buckled up?

The successful journey of a team provides success for each member of the team.

Step Ten: Defensive driving

It's not about your rights; it's about your responsibility.

DETOURS ON THE ROAD TO SUCCESS AND THE PLAN TO WORK AROUND OR THROUGH THE DETOURS

FEAR OF FAILURE
Achieve Quick Wins to demonstrate the vision.
There is no surer way to remove doubt or fear
than through the observation of success.

FORCED FAILURE
Acknowledge and reaffirm your commitment to the vision.
Once your team knows that you are committed to their success
they will commit to your vision.

FALSE FRIENDSHIP
Analyze intentions and return your focus to the vision.
Don't let flattery cause you to forget your focus.

FALSE FACTS
Admonish and proceed with your vision.
The proof of your character comes through in the lives of those on whom
you have an impact.

FOUR QUALITIES FOR A LEADERSHIP TEAM

COMMON PRINCIPLES
Common Principles are needed everywhere, but are not common in everyone: honesty, integrity, character, ethics, teamwork, motivation, and respect.

ENVIRONMENTAL EXPERIENCE
Those who have learned from the mistakes—their own or others'—are better prepared to lead than those who have never experienced mistakes at all.

PRACTICAL SUCCESSFUL BACKGROUND
Leaders with a history of success have developed a habit of working hard to achieve their success.

DIVERSE STRENGTHS
All of us are smarter than one of us.

FOUR SOURCES FOR RECRUITING A LEADERSHIP TEAM

- Current team members
- People you know from past experience
- Internal referrals
- External recruiting

BRIAN'S RESEARCH ON SBC

WHAT IS THE PURPOSE OF MY TEAM?

To deliver small-business accounting software that generates good revenue and profits, while fulfilling customer's needs.

WHAT ARE THE CONDITIONS IN AND AROUND MY TEAM?

How is the general economy? Businesses must control costs. Any product that a company purchases must generate savings that are greater than the price of the product.

How is the small-business industry? Small businesses are the backbone of the economy. There is enormous opportunity to provide the right accounting software to help small business succeed. Competition is not based on features—those are must haves. Competition is based on ease of use.

How is SBC competing in the industry? SBC is innovating and creating products that no one else is selling.

How should SBC compete in the industry? SBC should imitate when following success, and innovate when defining success.

How is SBC approaching its customers? SBC is generating sales by bringing in the most new customers with the most new products.

How should SBC approach its customers? SBC should focus on providing its customers with products they need and not finding customers for the products they have.

What are customers saying about SBC? SBC has tools with unique capabilities, but there are late deliveries, too many errors, and they are hard to learn.

What are employees saying about SBC? They are receiving confusing direction on product expectations, unrealistic delivery dates, and projects assignments that are out of their area of expertise.

BRIAN'S VISION AND QUICK WINS

SBC Small Business Accounting
Software Group Vision

We will fulfill our customers' small-business accounting needs by delivering software that we are proud to put the SBC name on: **S**imple to use, **B**y the promised due date, and **C**omprehensive.

We will deliver solutions to our customers' accounting needs by being:

- Expert listeners and learners so we understand our customer's needs.
- Expert organizers so we focus on the right priorities.
- Expert programmers so we develop the simplest solution possible.
- Expert project managers so we deliver error free and on time.

SBC Small-Business Accounting
Software Group Quick Wins

We will implement the following initiatives to put us on the path to achieve our vision:

- Establish a partnership with sales to develop an understanding of our customers' needs and a process to jointly discuss solutions.
- Establish a product and sales prioritization committee to jointly set and track product deliveries.
- Establish a process to assign the right programmer with the right skill set to the right piece of the product development project.
- Establish a training program to ensure that our programmers have the skills needed to deliver the products needed.
- Establish a process to ensure that all software is certified as error free before delivery.

Made in the USA
Middletown, DE
30 January 2015